EAST WITH ENSA

EAST WITH ENSA

Entertaining the Troops in the Second World War

Catharine Wells

The Radcliffe Press
London · New York

Published in 2001 by The Radcliffe Press
6 Salem Road, London W2 4BU
175 Fifth Avenue, New York NY 10010

In the United States and Canada
distributed by St Martin's Press
175 Fifth Avenue, New York NY 10010

ISBN 1–86064–718–9

A full CIP record for this book is available from the British Library
A full CIP record for this book is available from the Library of Congress

Library of Congress Catalog card: available

Typeset in Sabon by Oxford Publishing Services, Oxford
Printed and bound in Great Britain by MPG Books Ltd, Bodmin

IN MEMORY OF MY BROTHER MICHAEL MARKS WHO DIED
IN ACTION DURING THE SECOND WORLD WAR

Contents

Contents

Illustrations

Acronyms and Abbreviations

ADC	aide-de-camp
At	(member of the) Auxiliary Territorial Service
CO	Commanding Officer
ENSA	Entertainment's National Services Association
GI	US serviceman
NAAFI	Navy, Army, Air Force Institute
OC	officer in command
RAF	Royal Air Force
TAB	typhoid, paratyphoid A, paratyphoid B (vaccine)
tet. tox.	tetanus toxin
Wren	member of the Women's Royal Naval Service
YWCA	Young Women's Christian Association

Glossary

baksheesh	a gratuity
chokidar	night watchman
fellahin	peasants
gallabiyeh	long flapping robe worn by men
jildi jow	go quickly
kukri	knive with a curved blade that broadens towards the point, especially as used by Gurkhas
malesh	it does not matter/we could not care less
memsahib	term of respect used of a European married woman
sahib	form of address or title placed after a man's name or designation, used as a mark of respect
shtana schwiar	wait a bit
shufty	show (as in verb to show)
tarbush	felt or cloth brimless cap resembling the fez, usually red and often with a silk tassel, worn by Muslim men
tiki	very good (as a form of praise)
wallah	man (usually in some specialized connection)

1

Drury Lane, 1943

T he Theatre Royal, Drury Lane is in wartime dress: outside, instead of gigantic posters announcing some colossal musical production, with the names of the stars twinkling in lights overhead, today the boards, work-manlike and unostentatious, simply stated that here was the headquarters of the Entertainment's National Services Asso-ciation (ENSA), under the auspices of the Navy, Army, Air Force Institute (NAAFI).

Arriving at the main entrance, where in prewar days theatre patrons in evening dress had swept up the flight of steps to take their places in the stalls, boxes or royal circle, you were now confronted by an official and made to fill up a white pass stating your name and business before going any further. The front part of the theatre had been taken over entirely by the 'overseas' section. There, in the pillared and thickly carpeted entrance hall, wooden partitions had been rigged up enclosing the offices of Messrs Campbell, Leslie and Stanley.

Inside these offices, on the partition walls, hung huge maps showing the parts of the world to which ENSA was sending shows in the autumn of 1943 — the Middle East, Italy, the Far East and the west coast of Africa. Shows did not start to go to India until the Christmas of that year.

Whenever I had to visit those offices my eye would be irresistibly drawn to those plotted charts on the wall; in fact

1

my attention would keep wandering from what Mr Campbell, Mr Leslie or Mr Stanley might be saying, while my eyes roved from Cyprus to Syria to Persia, each causing a tingle of excitement to run through me — and finally to Cairo, our goal, and for me the most magical name of them all.

* * *

The Drury Lane stage — one of the finest and most historic in London — was now boarded up to reduce its size to that of an average camp theatre. Those coming for auditions, and they flowed in all day and every day, had to perform their acts inside the boarded-off section, though the gigantic spaciousness of the real stage spread temptingly all round them, especially temptingly for dancers. Day in day out and at all hours, the stage piano tinkled as singers, crooners, dancers and hoofers followed by comedians, acrobats and accordionists duly went through their routines before a small group of directors sitting in the stalls, who were hardly noticeable among that great waste of empty seats, yet were disagreeably and unavoidably there.

The wardrobe was on the top floor and, as with all theatrical wardrobes, it seethed with bustle and overwork. Harassed looking women with tired eyes behind spectacles called each other 'dear' or 'darling' to cover up their ever increasing irritability.

Somewhere below the stalls, you dived down a passage to get yourself vaccinated and inoculated, with TAB and tet. tox. being compulsory for overseas personnel. Outside the doctor's room waited a long queue: you attached yourself to the end, received your jabs in due course and were told to come back at the same time the following week and to go to an institute in the Euston Road to be 'done' for yellow fever and typhus.

Across the road opposite the stage door we went to other offices to fill in countless forms on which we had to state our name, age and the stability of our British nationality (an Italian grandmother might cause trouble). We then went back again across the street to the theatre to visit Mr Abingdon in his office by the stage door to discuss the matter of coupons for stage costumes.

One went round to the front again for a conversation with the 'pool' manager. All artistes who were not going out in 'shows' were in the 'pool', to be placed in companies on arrival in Cairo. The manager had a list of necessary and helpful articles, which he advised us to get for a year overseas.

'I should get your tin trunk from Mosses, and you can buy good sun and sand glasses at Gamages, and that's the place for water bottles. Then it's got down here "toupee, mackintosh, soap, make up, roll of toilet paper", though how one roll's supposed to last you a whole year I don't know.'

* * *

Mr Leslie had told me that he wanted me to be ready in a fortnight's time to sail with the next convoy. Never before or since have I spent such a hectic time, in addition to nine performances a week with the Kyasht Ballet at the Whitehall Theatre, preparing to teach my parts to other members and rushing up to Hampstead to finish sitting for my future father-in-law who was painting my portrait. His son, stationed in Syria, had first articulated the idea of my joining ENSA and coming out to the Middle East.

That fortnight I kept up a continual rush, from signing papers at 'Drury Lane' to the Whitehall for rehearsals, to the Board of Trade to collect my special allowance of coupons, to the shops to buy all that I feverishly could, back to the doctor's for another needle to be stuck into me and from there on to the evening performance.

One Wednesday morning after a portrait sitting, I rushed down to Drury Lane in a taxi with my passport, which had

3

to be handed in that day. With a matinée at half past two and no time to lose, I tore up the front steps and into the entrance hall only to realize with horror a few minutes later that I had left my passport in the taxi.

What a horrible vision it engendered! I imagined being unable to get it back for days, perhaps weeks, the convoy sailing and all the frantic preparation having being to no purpose. However, I was lucky. The taxi driver had done what all good taxi drivers should do; he had looked inside his cab, found the passport and handed it in at the stage door. The stage doorman had phoned through to all the departments of the theatre to report the find and to trace the owner; and so, whichever department I went into that day, I was greeted with, 'Oh yes, you're Miss Marks who left her passport in the taxi.'

Another mishap occurred on my way to a security talk in the Little Fortune Theatre across the street. Being late as usual, I was running, and, turning the corner, slipped on the wet pavement and fell flat on my back right at the feet of Mr Stanley and the lecturer who were just arriving. Mr Stanley helped me up, saying kindly, if somewhat humiliatingly, 'You naughty girl.'

Altogether, I did not feel that I had started off by making a very good impression with ENSA, one way and another.

* * *

We were all told to be at the theatre at nine o'clock on the evening of our 'D-Day' — Saturday 16 October 1943. We had brought all our baggage down in advance that morning and had been asked not to bring friends or relatives to see us off: for security reasons we must leave as unobtrusively as possible. We were not ever told from which London terminus we would be leaving, let alone to which port we would be travelling. This, of course, merely heightened our feeling of excitement. It seemed extraordinary to be leaving

4

for an adventure across the world, and for an absence from home of at least a year, by simply stepping into a bus at the end of the road, quite alone, and with only a carrier bag and travelling rug under one arm. The whole thing seemed completely unreal: it made me feel as if I had probably come at the wrong time or on the wrong day, for everything felt so absolutely wrong. It was a relief when, having stepped off the bus at the Aldwych corner and turned up dark St Catherine Street towards the theatre, a fellow member of the 'pool' joined me from behind — a calm, solid and reassuring American man wearing glasses and homburg hat drawled observations on the time and weather and speculated on when we should be leaving.

Inside the dimly lit theatre there was an air of anticipation. Young women in slacks with their hair tied up in turbans, and men in heavy travelling coats with a rug thrown over one arm queued up outside Mr Stanley's office to be handed back their passports and inoculation papers, which were now all in order for the voyage. Groups sat about on the stairs, smoking and talking. Others were sticking ENSA labels marked with a red X onto their baggage. There was an elderly woman with a birdcage and one young woman was lugging along a gramophone. This was the largest party ENSA had ever sent overseas — there were more than a hundred of us: nine complete shows and 20 people in the pool. Out of the whole lot I had only previously known one — Robertson, a tiny doll-like young woman who did a dancing act with her partner Caroline. I did not see either of them to begin with, so I sat down on one of the foyer sofas and talked to a Mrs Paine, a pleasant warm-hearted woman who was travelling out with her comedian husband. They had an act together. I have no idea what we talked about; it was all just marking time. We were not told how long we would have to wait that night in the half-lit chilly theatre. Some people were depressingly exaggerating that they would not take us to the station until the morning.

'Where do we spend the night then?' 'Oh, they'll bung us in some air-raid shelter probably.'

The lady with the birdcage began to cheer up her neighbours with a coy little story about an oyster losing its pearl.

Eventually, we were all called onto the stage and told to assemble in our various groups. The stage seemed larger than ever in the gloomy half-light; everyone was expectant, impatient to be gone. Mr Stanley began a rollcall, running through the shows in turn, each company filing out after their names had been called to the coaches outside the stage door — *Happy Hikers*, *Swing Time*, *Ladies in Waiting* and finally the 'pool'. We were the last to leave that vast and now empty stage from where, perhaps, the ghosts of David Garrick and Peg Woffington were waving us farewell and Godspeed. We were among the last to file out, shake hands with Mr Leslie at the stage door, and climb up into the dark and uncomfortable coaches waiting outside.

It was then just about midnight — the American with the spectacles and homburg hat was checking up on the time. We thought our destination would probably be Euston, but no, the procession of coaches swung off westwards. It would not be one of the northern stations then. Could it be Paddington? Surely we would not be leaving from a southern port. We were more mystified than ever. As we passed through Piccadilly Circus the sirens began to wail — that was London's farewell to us.

2

Unknown Destination

After turning down Piccadilly, crossing Hyde Park Corner, and from there running down through Knightsbridge to Kensington alongside the moonlit and shadowy park, we eventually landed up at Addison Road station, Olympia.

Two or three carriages were waiting at the platform and into these everyone hurried to find themselves seats. The 'pool', having come down in the final coach, was of course the last to arrive and so had the most difficulty finding room. I had joined Caroline and Robertson in the coach, but we had to separate and I found myself next to a member of the *Swing Time* band, who was kind enough to give up his corner to me. It was an open-type carriage with a passageway down the middle and little tables on either side. All around sat the members of *Let's Have a Party*, among them the woman with the birdcage, with her strident voice and swarthy gypsy looks. Beside her sat her diminutive sharp-featured husband and opposite sat a tiny, elderly lady — also a bit of a gypsy — and her tall beautiful golden-haired daughter Rowena. Then there was bald and spectacled Albert, and bobbed-hair, fresh-complexioned Edith, who looked as if she would be more at home on a farm than on the stage. I tried to puzzle out what they all did as they busied themselves with thermos flasks and sandwiches, spread themselves out and tried to get comfortable. ENSA had provided everybody with lunch boxes, with the warning that as the length of the journey was not going to be divulged, these boxes must be made to 'last out'. However, having poked their noses inside and tasted a very 'wartime' meal, most people promptly decided that the contents were uneatable, so returned to their own marmite sandwiches.

My neighbour, however, made quite a lot of headway with his lunch box before leaning back in his seat with folded arms and starting to doze.

* * *

Our carriages remained motionless for what seemed like hours before we were shunted off somewhere, where we stopped again with creakings and clatterings of couplings, reshunted, and then spent another long period of dreary waiting. The carriage was too badly lit to read and a party of card players further down the coach, including somebody with a piercing hyena laugh, successfully prevented anyone from getting any sleep. I sat there feeling desperately miserable. I had been warned against the 'Oh why did I ever say I'd go?' feeling at the beginning of a long journey, but although I was prepared to feel like this, it failed to make the dim and stuffy carriage, interminably shunting up and down on a limbo of railway sidings and crowded with seemingly totally unsympathetic people after my friends in the ballet world, any more bearable.

* * *

But when dawn broke and the train was moving swiftly, I gently lifted the blinds and looked out on a delicate white mist trailing over dew-sodden grass with hazy outlines of trees in the distance. I felt at once as refreshed as if I had bathed in the dew and excitement welled up within me again. The rest of the people in the carriage, who were waking up, stiff and yawning, became interesting and amusing to watch and to listen to. The *Let's Have a Party* crowd were organizing a sweepstake, making bets on which ports we were most likely to be going from. I did not feel that whoever was betting on Southampton or Bristol would have much of a chance because, from the character of the country outside, we were clearly travelling northwards — it looked unmistakably like Yorkshire to me. However, some security-conscious person suggested that just to put everyone off the scent we would probably be kept travelling round England for a day or two.

'They said we must make our lunch boxes last.' This idea was probably from the same person who had thought of the air-raid shelter.

Presently, we drew into a large station and I was not surprised to see Sheffield written up on the boards. There was a stampede from the carriages to the refreshment room for cups of tea. Five minutes later a bell rang and the stampede returned; nearly everybody had been unsuccessful; they were empty-handed and complaining bitterly. The despised lunch boxes were grudgingly reopened.

Then it was to Liverpool station to which we had arrived and it was only midday. Again we had to pile into coaches that were waiting outside the station, where such a large crowd stood and gaped at us that we wondered what on earth all the previous security arrangements had been about.

* * *

Down we went to the docks, glimpsing the funnels of great ships above and between dreary grey buildings, into a shed where we hung about for a time over official matters such as handing in our ration books, then speedily through customs and into coaches again to be taken to the dockside and to our ships. We were promised lunch on board but found that we had to wait a couple of hours on the landing stage before it came to be ENSA's turn to climb the gangway. By the time we were eventually to get on board, lunch was long over and we actually sighed for the much-abused lunch boxes we had discarded in the railway carriage.

Everyone was very excited to see the ship. It seemed simply enormous, with its bows literally swarming with soldiers and sailors crowding against the rails of every deck. Its vastness imparted a strong feeling of security — such a monster as that could not possibly sink.

As we stood waiting in the vast, damp and chilly shed, truckload upon truckload of men kept arriving outside, were organized into lines and filed through the shed and up the gangway, each man weighted down with heavy equipment. We watched the great ship absorb them all into its side, hundreds upon hundreds of them. When the dockhands began to distribute peanuts out of huge sacks, we felt rather like a group of monkeys, but with our empty stomachs we were grateful for anything. They were also throwing peanuts up to the men swarming against the rails above. Scores of hands were outstretched to catch the bundles of nuts as they were tossed up.

A sailor's hat was knocked off and fell down into the gap between the ship and the quayside. One of the dockhands fished it out for him and threw it up; scores of hands shot out, but everybody missed the hat and it fell back into the sea again, only to be fished out and thrown up once more. This performance was repeated several times amid gusts of laughter, groans and jeers; it helped to pass the hours of waiting.

* * *

At last, at the very end, the members of ENSA (priority Z) were allowed to go on board. However, each young woman had the honour of being cheered by sailors as we walked up the gangway — it was a wonderful welcome.

Down below all was bustle and confusion, with everyone looking lost and bewildered and pushing in every direction. After a while I managed to discover which cabin I was supposed to go to and then, after more pushing against the throng and asking every likely looking person I saw, eventually arrived at the right number on the right deck.

I found that I had been allotted a bunk in a four-berthed cabin on B deck, which I was to share with three Rhythm Sisters, Anita, Clare and Pamela, the first two being genuinely related, the youngest, Pamela having only just joined them. Anita, the stronger-minded and better looking of the two sisters, was clearly the 'boss' of them all. Clare, far less of a stage type than her sister, seemed to have a softer easier disposition. Golden-haired Anita struck me as being rather strained and nervy: she had the responsibility of the act to bear. Pamela's large size and tremendous auburn coiffure, combined with a refined cockney accent put me off her to begin with, but later we became quite friendly. I found that she had plenty of common sense and very decided opinions, formed chiefly during her time as barmaid at a West End nightclub. She also had a real cockney sense of humour.

The cabin was of course tiny with the two extra bunks fitted into it, but it was fresh and clean looking with its new white paint in that particularly spruce 'board ship' way.

We unpacked, continually bumping behinds while bending over and apologizing politely. There was a drawer and shelf each, and a small portion of space in the hanging cupboard. Pamela and I agreed to sleep 'up' and the two sisters 'down'.

* * *

At half past six the first bell rang for dinner. All ENSA members were to go to the first sittings, with the nurses and the small group of RAF officers on board. All army officers were to go to the second sitting. This caused quite a lot of ill feeling. 'Why should the blasted RAF be the ones chosen to join the ladies?' But the army did have the advantage of getting up an hour later for breakfast in the morning.

The dining room was several decks below us, and as we walked down, the men on the lower decks came to the staircase to watch us go by. We felt sorry for them, crowded together as they were in their blacked-out and airless quarters.

In the dining room, I sat at a table with my three cabin mates. Everyone was commenting on the joy of eating white bread again and on the excellence of the food. It was not long of course before they were grumbling at it, but the first dinner at any rate was magnificent.

The *Marnix* was a Dutch ship and our waiters were Javanese. Small and brown, they moved about serving dishes with a kind of dreamy waddle. A remarkably handsome Dutch steward officer stood at the end of the room blandly smiling on the scene.

After dinner we went to the officers' lounge, but it was far too crowded for half the people in it to sit down on the bulky leather armchairs, and the air thick and horrible with smoke. A game of cards was going on among the RAF officers, which both Pamela and I were asked to join. The *Marnix* was to be a 'dry' ship, and it seemed incongruous to see RAF officers sitting sipping lemonade. The air buzzed with the voices of people getting acquainted and the smoke became thicker than ever and pricked one's eyeballs. I left early to go to the cabin and the partial privacy of my top bunk. The crowd and the atmosphere of the lounge had become overpowering and I was tired out from the long journey and hectic preceding weeks. It was delightful to slip between the cool sheets and let sleep slowly creep over my tired limbs. Even when, later on, Pamela started snoring, it could not keep me awake for long.

3

Winter Cruise

Next morning we were awakened at half past seven by a bugle call in the passage outside and we got dressed and washed in turn in the tiny cabin space. Nobody knew how many days we were to sit in Liverpool harbour, though of course everyone had his or her ideas.

After breakfast, we were summoned to the lounge for a little talk by the Dutch captain. He explained about the boat drill we would be having every day and about the importance of always carrying our life belts.

'Nothing has ever happened to this ship yet, though,' he concluded, 'and I don't see why anything ever should.' Dozens of hands made a dive to touch wood at this shocking boast.

Later on we had the first boat drill and from then onwards daily at two o'clock, disturbing everyone's siesta, we had to stand in the bitter Atlantic wind on the top deck in rows facing our appointed lifeboat. We stood there shivering and grumbling until, the inspection being over, the welcome bell rang and we could take off our lifebelts and go below.

* * *

Everyone was quickly becoming sociable and even on that first day sets were forming. Anita, Clare, Pamela and I had a rummy-playing set with a couple of young engineer subalterns — Chaiks, a good looking RAF dental officer, whose teeth were an advertisement to his profession; Captain Norfolk, an architect in private life; and, later on, a little handsome pipe-smoking member of the RAF named Denis who proved himself to be a regular lady killer. He had a little trick of taking his pipe out of his mouth and saying 'peep, peep' out of the corner, in a way that was considered to be very fetching.

* * *

The next morning, to our surprise, the diesel engines started to throb through the ship and we steamed out of Liverpool harbour. Everyone crowded up on deck to feel the keen sea air blowing in their faces and to lean on the rails and watch the great Atlantic rollers crashing themselves against the ship's side.

It was more exciting still when land appeared, grey mountains, on the horizon. We did not know whether it was the coast of Wales, Ireland, or the Isle of Man. I asked a Dutch navel officer if he would tell me. 'My middle name is Oyster' was the only reply I got.

It was a bit of an anti-climax when, after a while, the engines stopped drumming and the *Marnix* sat placidly on the water making no further headway, and more still when it turned round and started steaming back to Liverpool harbour. There were loud exclamations of disappointment when it was realized that this had been only a trial trip and that we were back in port once more.

However, it was not for long, for during the night we left again and made our way to Glasgow to join the rest of the convoy. It was a wonderful sight when they were all assembled, to stand on deck and see the great grey armoured ships all around us in formation. How proud and purposeful they appeared, and yet at the same time as impersonal as the pieces on a chessboard. It was hard to realize that they too were as crowded with human life as we were. Our position was last in the convoy, so the Armada streamed ahead and spread out on both sides of us.

* * *

Life on board ship, even in wartime, speedily forms itself into a pattern. We would start the morning, when breakfast was over, by walking up on deck — eight times round to make a mile, which Clare and Pamela set themselves to do regularly each day. Later, physical training and early-morning skipping came into fashion on the top deck. It was good to be up in the buoyant sea breezes after the stuffiness of the sealed cabin all night.

Later on, when the army officers came trooping up from their second sitting breakfast, there would be relaxed promenades, conversational leanings against the rails and chatty interruptions to whatever book one was trying to read unnoticed on some back seat.

If the morning were wet and cold, there would probably follow a rubber of rummy in the lounge; and a queue would begin to form for cigarettes and drinks — only lemonade of course — when the bar opened before lunch. I did get a drink or two later on in the voyage with one of the Dutch officers who were allowed to have grog in their cabins.

* * *

Various people had morning jobs to do. The officers had to visit their men; Captain Norfolk, with whom I had made friends, had to think up what security talks to give; and Anita and Clare had to rehearse Pamela in their numbers. There were also classes in Urdu being held in the mornings because the majority of the troops on board, as well as the nurses, were bound for India.

I retired for some time during the day to practise my barre work in our cabin, which was very cramped but just possible. It amused me to see if I could do a plié in the middle of the floor with the ship rolling and not fall over.

After lunch, of course, we had the tiresome boat drill and when that was finished I would escape from further rummy in the lounge to my top bunk and a book. The evenings were sociable and various volunteers from the ENSA ranks gave several impromptu concerts. I was relieved to find that no dancers — save for one woman who tap danced — came forward, for I myself had no wish to perform in a tiny space and on a heaving floor when I knew that I could not possibly give of my best. However, I enjoyed listening to Albert, my opposite neighbour in the railway carriage, play Liszt, and the red-haired Edith sing 'Annie Laurie' and other old favourites in a rich contralto voice, and to Mr Paine telling gags in between items.

Later on, other amusements in the shape of a spelling bee and a brains trust were organized, but the moon, which grew romantically fuller as we drew further south and the nights became warmer, provided the greatest draw of all.

* * *

Having my moonlight waiting for me in Cairo, I avoided the decks and was nearly always first in my bunk at night — ready to hear how my cabin mates' love affairs were coming along. Anita and the RAF dental officer with the magnificent teeth had fallen for one another and she would come back to the cabin with shining eyes to tell us all about it. They were engaged before the end of the voyage and theirs was possibly the only one of many *Marnix* engagements that eventually ended in a wedding. Though Chaiks was married, he had been separated for a couple of years and seemed to be serious about Anita. Not so little Denny, however, who successfully destroyed Pamela's peace of mind.

'I've got it,' she moaned, 'I've got it bad.' Denny was married too, but of course did not love his wife and had many a tale of woe about her, but at the same time she saved him from falling into any matrimonial traps.

Oh, those poor misunderstood husbands, how often one was to meet them in the Middle East and listen to their hard luck stories about their wives at home — stories told for sympathy and kisses from gullible young women.

Poor Pamela, at first she had cold-shouldered little Denny. 'He'll say', she would tell us, 'that if I won't go out on the deck with him he'll "go winking".' 'What's that?' we asked. Pamela explained that it was a secret and meant that RAF officers on the loose at night would wink at a woman who caught their eye; then if she winked back she would have to kiss him. But it was not long before Pamela decided that she must be the only woman at whom little Denny might wink.

These certainly were not the only romances going on; there were dozens of them and the infection spread rapidly. I had agreed to teach the physical training officer the sword dance in return for lessons in jujitsu, but after two sessions with the swords, he fell victim to the popular complaint and retired in a state of melancholia. So we never got into jujitsu, which was disappointing. When the course of the convoy took us out some way into the Atlantic, the sea became rough and people started going down with *mal de mer*. I got used to seeing them staggering along the corridors looking pale and miserable and felt sorry for them in a slightly superior way until someone remarked how rotten I looked and I was immediately as sick as a cat.

* * *

After a few day of this, however, the weather turned surprisingly warm, and the sea became quite calm, the convoy shifted course eastwards, and one afternoon the Straits of Gibraltar came into sight.

Nearly everyone was gathered on the top deck sunbathing. The members of ENSA had blossomed out in bathing costumes, sunsuits and summer dresses. It seemed hard that the other women on board, the nurses, had to remain in their uniforms and they certainly resented it.

'Indecent little bitch,' Pamela overheard one of them remark as she walked past in her two-piece sunsuit.

It had been a very pleasant afternoon. Some of the people on board had brought their guitars up on deck. This is a lovely instrument to listen to at sea while watching the waves ripple by. The sun has been so deliciously warm — we had begun to feel that we really were missing the English winter — and everyone had been lazy and contented. Except for the fact that all the men were in uniform and there were guns on board, the *Marnix* might have been a pleasure cruiser.

* * *

And now here was Gibraltar, the threshold of the Mediterranean, and the convoy was forming itself into a single file to pass through the straits with the required amount of neutral waters to be allowed for on either side.

I was more impressed by my first sight of the coast of Africa than than I was by the Rock of Gibraltar, which I believe needs to be seen from underneath if one is fully to appreciate its grandeur.

Those lion-like African mountains looked magnificent across the sea and later when the sun set behind them in a crimson sky and their shapes stood out — black and forbidding in bulk with clean-cut strong outlines — I felt a burning excitement, the power of Africa, and sensed the thousands of miles of land that rolled back from the sea behind the mountains.

I was standing with a member of the Anglo–Persian Oil Company, of whom there were quite a few on board, and we were looking for the Atlas Mountains. Pamela, in sunbathing attire, planted herself in front of us, legs astride.

'I fancy I see the Atlas Mountains now,' murmured my companion.

It was hard to leave the wonderful new coast and go down to dinner, but when the meal was over everyone crowded up on deck again to watch the moon rise from behind the African mountains and shine across the sea to the ship, making a shimmering white pathway, lying like mercury on the water. It looked entrancing and I longed to leap overboard and dance along it. Phosphorescence appeared and disappeared like magic close to the ship's side, and the water swished softly past.

4

Attack and Escape in Lifeboats

I t was on a clear bright afternoon a day or two later that I was having a talk with one of the gunners on deck. Very young, very fair and very English, he told me how he had been brought up on a farm in Lancashire and hoped to go back there after the war.

'I suppose,' I said, 'that now we are out of the Atlantic, the dangerous part of the voyage is over?'

'No,' he answered, 'as a matter of fact it is just beginning because they can send planes over so easily from the south of France and Italy, and then later on from bases in Crete.'

Apart from the first night at sea, I had hardly thought of submarines and not at all of air attacks, but even this information, while I was not counting the days before we would be in Cairo, did not worry me over much. And yet, soon after six the following evening, when the bell had been rung for first dinner, the air attack signal went off. That morning at breakfast I had said: 'I'm sure something has happened to me on 6 November, but I can't remember what.' I shall certainly always remember now.

* * *

Anita, Clare, Pamela and I were about to leave our cabin for dinner. We knew there was roast chicken on the menu for

the first time, so were punctual. I remembered that the
gunner had said, 'In an air attack you are safest on B deck,'
which was exactly where we were now. Those who had
already gone down to dinner were sent straight up again.

We put on our 'Mae West' lifebelts, looking rather self-
consciously at each other as if such precautions were absurd
but one must obey the rules. The next minute there was a
roar of planes overhead and the guns on the deck above
gave out such a tremendous thundering that we shrank back
against the walls of the cabin.

We felt the ship put on all the speed of which it was
capable, zigzagging from side to side, while the guns kept up
their uproar overhead. The noise was so loud that it seemed
impossible to believe that this was not the end of all things;
the next minute there came by far the most violent explosion
of them all; the lights went out, the floor of the cabin reeled
and Anita shrieked, 'God! They've got us.'

The next minute I expected water to come pouring in, to
be sucked under, unable to escape, overpowered, drowned,
and I wildly longed and prayed to be allowed to live.

* * *

Slowly, slowly, the horror retreated and I realized that I was
still alive, within the cabin with Anita, Clare and Pamela,
and that outside the door crowds were pushing past to get
to the stairway leading up to A deck.

We left the cabin and were swept along with the crowd.
All the electrical power had gone, we were in total darkness
and the microphones were dead so no orders could be given
out through them. Nobody knew if the danger was immi-
nent, if we were to go to our boat stations or to remain
below, but as the crowd surged up the stairway the sailors
on deck advised us to stay below for the time being anyway,
for the barrage was still very heavy. I had a brief glimpse of
an angry sky, red hot with explosions, before being swept

back with the press of people. Once again I found myself in our cabin with Anita and Clare, and Pamela who had never left it. The *Marnix* had straightened up by now and the firing overhead began to die down.

Pamela announced that it was disgraceful how everyone had gone pushing up on deck, that of course we had not really been hit, that the bomb, or whatever had been dropped, had only fallen in the sea close by us. These rumours that were going around of our having to leave the ship were all nonsense. This talk was perhaps a good thing in its way, but Pamela or no Pamela I put on my big coat, and fumbled in the darkness for the specially packed 'panic bag' so as to be ready just in case.

Presently the crowd started to press outside again, and the word was passed that we were to go to the boats. Pamela came with us this time, though declaring loudly that 'surely we wouldn't actually have to leave the ship,' and that 'there couldn't possible be any real danger.'

'Oh no, Miss,' said a sailor overhearing her, 'they're only dropping butterflies.'

Women were already being helped over the side of the ship into our lifeboat by the time we reached it. There was no trace of panic except among the Javanese, who had been detailed to row the boats and who were now screaming with terror and being quite hopeless.

One by one a squint-eyed petty officer gave us a hand and helped us into the boat. There were 50 in each and we were edged so tightly together we could hardly move a limb. Our 50 were nearly all ENSA women; there were two or three ENSA men, a soldier with a bad arm from the ship's hospital, the petty officer and a Dutch officer to act as captain.

It was a horrible sensation when they began to lower the boat down to the water. At one moment we caught against the side of the ship and were nearly all tipped out into the inky sea below. Then another boatload drifted underneath us and it seemed as if we would land right on top of them. It moved out of the way only just in time and we arrived safely on the surface of the water. Big David of ENSA took an oar, the petty officer two others, while the wounded soldier insisted on having the fourth, though rowing with his bad arm must have been extremely painful for him. The Dutch officer steered and gave orders. They pushed us away from the ship's side, and we drifted out into the dark rocking sea.

* * *

Several of the women began to feel sick from the intensified motion of the small boat and also probably from the shock. Next to me was wedged little red-haired Deidré, whom I had noticed before and rather disliked because she had such an aggrieved, complaining expression, but now, ashen pale and just having been violently sick, she stood in the middle of the boat smiling bravely, her long red hair blowing back in the wind. I put an arm round her to give her more support.

All around us, little boats were bobbing on the water, each packed tightly, and not many yards away the *Marnix* itself loomed up, lying there, large and gaunt in the moonlight, a sitting target for any aeroplane that might return. I think that more than one of us was thinking this and listening for the drone of a returning plane to come swooping down and machinegun us in the boats, and I know that I for one was relieved when clouds drew over the moon and it began to rain. Coat collars were turned up, golden-haired Della tied a scarf over her head and someone encouragingly remarked that 'now we should all look far more like survivors when we were eventually picked up.'

A sudden light gleamed out from a boat across the water, and a roar of 'put out that cigarette' came from all sides. Then the darkness seemed to envelop us and cut us off completely from the other boats, and we drifted on in a timeless unreality. People spoke at times, but not very much. There was a general bewailment over the missed roast chicken for dinner and, to a lesser degree, over all the personal property left on board. I must say that I was thinking very sadly of my new trunk, especially of my skip filled with theatrical costumes and ballet shoes, which meant far more to me than my ordinary clothes.

* * *

At last our captain started shouting orders from the stern and we made out the shape of another boat moving towards us and then, by degrees, the larger outlines of a destroyer pitching up and down a little further off.

We were thrown a rope from the small boat and, after a trying period of waiting while the people off another lifeboat were being heaved on board, we were drawn up to the destroyer. Someone remarked that there probably would not be room for us as well, for the destroyer certainly did not look very big. However, we were pulled in alongside and orders in broad American were being yelled from above, telling us that when the destroyer, which was riding up and down on the water like a seesaw, dipped towards our boat, we were to jump up and cling tightly to the net that had been thrown over the deck rail and so be carried up out of the boat as the ship rose and then heaved over the rail on to the deck.

We went up two at a time. It was quite breathtaking waiting for the dip of the net, clutching it and then feeling yourself lifted up into midair while dozens of helpful arms outstretched to pull you over on to the deck, with Yankee voices saying 'come along, step on it sister' in your ear. I felt my head reel as I walked along the deck and staggered against the side, but I still had my 'panic bag' tightly gripped in one hand.

We were shepherded down below and into a packed low-roofed saloon where coffee was being ladled out. There was none left when it came to my turn and, as I was suddenly feeling ravenously hungry, I was only too glad to accept a piece of chocolate from the squint-eyed petty officer. He told me details of the attack, how the aerial torpedo that had hit us had gone into the engine room, right through the heart of the ship, but how none of the men down there had been killed. He felt sure that the *Marnix* would sink, though it might not be for some time, adding with deep conviction that we had all had a wonderful escape. 'It was the Lord,' he said very simply at the end.

* * *

Later, all the women on board were taken to rest in the officers' cabins. I found myself in with two or three of the nurses and a Wren, a survivor off another ship in the convoy that had been hit. The owner of the cabin came in and invited us to make ourselves at home, putting out packets of Camel cigarettes, piles of American magazines and later bringing in armfuls of blankets. I pulled off my dress and climbed up into a top bunk with one of the nurses, lying head to feet.

The cabin was right forward in the bows of the ship. We seemed to be going very fast, and rocking from side to side so violently, that I was terrified lest the ship was over-full and we should rock right over. I could not sleep and turned from side to side under the blanket. The woman in the bunk below kept on being sick and half crying to herself.

* * *

All of a sudden there came a horrible shudder through the ship and a blue light went on in the corridor outside. A minute later an officer came in to tell us not to worry, that nothing had happened, only that a submarine was following us and we were dropping depth charges. Now I really felt frightened — I could no longer lie on the bunk. I got up and dressed and sat on the floor by the door, listening and waiting, longing to go up on deck into the fresh air while the destroyer, rocking madly, tore on through the night.

5

Survivors Landing in North Africa

Morning arrived and sunshine flooded the ship. We felt the engines stop and the anchor lowered, and came up on deck to see if we had arrived somewhere. The destroyer was lying peacefully outside a harbour bay. Across the sparkling blue water, a little town of whitewashed red-roofed houses clustered at the quayside and climbed up the hillside in terraces. All round the bay the hills, green and thickly vegetated, rose up out of the sea. The whole scene looked so attractive and inviting that I longed to go ashore and explore as soon as possible, and I think everyone had the greatest desire to plant his or her feet on the solid earth again. However, this was not to be until the late afternoon because permission for us to land had first to be obtained from the port authorities and they seemed to need a whole day in which to make up their minds about whether or not permission should be given. So we all went below for breakfast, served in a hot steamy atmosphere by very dark-skinned waiters. It consisted of very sweet cereal, excellent coffee and a type of waffle pancake. I felt as though I were taking part in an American film — it was just the type of breakfast you see them enjoying on the screen.

Later a service of thanksgiving was broadcast over the loudspeakers, which unfortunately was rather unimpressive because nobody could hear it properly. Then we sat on deck in groups and talked; time dragged until at last the awaited permission arrived; the destroyer then steamed into the harbour and drew up at the dockside.

* * *

Disembarking was a slow business with so many on board, though of course nobody had any luggage difficulties. It was exciting to be on African soil for the first time, though the excitement wore off as time went by. Evening came and we were still waiting about on the now chilly dockside. Later on we were taken to a filthy shed that smelt appallingly in every corner and served soup-like tea and buns from a NAAFI van. Nobody refused; we were all too hungry. The destroyer's rations had been unable to go further than a sandwich each for lunch.

We learnt that this was Phillipville on the North African coast, east of Algiers. Now that we were actually in the place it was strange how much less attractive it seemed than the view of it across the bay had suggested. We were all longing to be taken somewhere clean and comfortable where we could have a bath and sleep, but there was a lot more hanging about to be endured before plans were worked out and it was decided which groups were to go where.

The military personnel were all taken off to camps outside the town on the coast, and the sisters were sent to the hospital. One party of ENSA people was sent to the ENSA hostel at Constantine and another to Bone. Those remaining at Phillipville were divided into two groups, one lot, the more fortunate ones, going to what had formerly been a hotel on the front, the other group, including my cabin companions and me, to the hostel.

* * *

I shall never forget either the hostel or how miserable I was during the week I spent there. My feelings were certainly exacerbated by my having no clothes, save those I stood up in, and the depressing thought of having to stay there, perhaps for weeks, with our arrival in Cairo indefinitely postponed. But what a horrible place it was!

It had formerly been a brothel. A guard had to be posted at the door to prevent any of the former clientele from coming up the dirty narrow staircase; it was not, however, as bad as the hostel at Bone, which had not only been a brothel itself but it also still had a flourishing concern going next door. One of the women off the ship who stayed in the Bone hostel told me later that as she turned into the street one evening to go home, a soldier gave her a friendly warning: 'I shouldn't go down there, Miss.'

'I have to,' she replied, 'I live there.' This was the actress Diana Dors.

Our hostel, besides being dirty, smelt abominably from the bad drains. The first night I spent in a small room lying on a blanket on the stone floor with a young woman called Maisy Marlow, while the three Rhythm Sisters squashed themselves into the bed. Of course we knew that this sort of discomfort could not be helped and nobody grumbled about it or about there not being any hot water in which to wash. I also meekly accepted the 'pool' manager Bobby's instructions, when he came round reorganizing things the next day, that I was in future to share a room with Madame, the hostel proprietress, her daughter and, I believe, her aunt, but when I went into the room the smell was so sickening that I decided I would rather sleep in the street than in there.

Fortunately, I did not have to go to this extreme, for a major we met at the officers' club where we went for meals lent me a camp bed, which I put up in one of the women's rooms.

The officers' club, despite the beautiful bougainvillaea hanging over its door, was as dirty and as sordid as the hostel. The British sergeant in charge did not seem to bother, or perhaps he had given up, and the Italian servants were bone-lazy.

The tablecloths on which the food was served were so filthy that after a few days Maisy and I could bear it no longer, so we carried them up to a wash house on the roof where we persuaded two Italians who were there to light up the coppers so that we could boil and scrub the dozen or so tablecloths. While we were doing this, the two servants lounged around and grinned at us as if we were crazy. After a hard morning's work, the cloths were still a pale grey, but at least we felt that we must have destroyed quite a few germs.

Travelling abroad I do not find, as so many English people seem to find, that dirt and smells ruin everything else for me. I have talked to so many officers and men in 'after the show' messes who have been unable to see the beauty and attraction of foreign towns because they are conscious only of the dirt — 'Naples! You can have it, nothing but filth and smells,' I have heard on more than one occasion. How smugly it was said, too, as if there were something knowing and superior about debunking such places when really the speakers were to be deeply pitied for having noses with which to smell but no eyes with which to see.

However, I must admit that although even Eastern dirtiness does not mar beauty for me if I myself am living in clean conditions, it is a different matter to be cheek by jowl with the dirt in a smelly sordid hostel. I felt thoroughly nauseated all the time I was in Phillipville, but if others have found it an interesting and attractive place I am quite ready to believe them. Personally, I loathed it.

In case all this is giving a bad impression of ENSA's overseas accommodation, I must add that this was the first and last time I had to stay in a place like the Phillipville hostel. In the towns, ENSA people were always accommodated in the best hotels or in well-run hostels, and when we were put up in camps, the accommodation — though naturally a bit rough — was always spotlessly clean.

The truth of the matter was, I believe, that until very recently North Africa had been under German occupation. There was a definite feeling of hostility toward the British. Probably ENSA had just had to do the best it could and we were unlucky enough to get shipwrecked and to land up in that part of the world. Although the news of our arrival was all over the town in no time, none of the residents came forward with any offers of hospitality or clothing for us.

* * *

The morning after our arrival, I went off with Anita, Clare, Pamela and Maisy on a shopping expedition to see if it was possible to buy a change of underwear in the town. Maisy wanted some shoes too. Poor soul, she had been getting ready to take part in a show when the alarm had gone off, and had had to leave the ship in full stage makeup, slacks, a coat and a pair of bedroom slippers. I wanted some shoes, too, for my high-heeled ones were most uncomfortable to walk in over the cobbled streets. But the sandals we succeeded in buying were hopelessly made and collapsed in one day. We found that there was practically nothing to be bought in the shops and the few things there were required coupons. However, one shopkeeper produced some little striped panties and announced triumphantly, 'black market'.

None of us felt like being squeamish about that and we all hastily bought some, and afterwards coffee was brought in on a dainty little tray, which — being the first time any of us had experienced this oriental form of courtesy at the close of a purchase — intrigued us very much.

The next day the three Rhythm Sisters moved to a private house they had been told of through friends. They had to sleep on the floor, but preferred it to the hostel. Maisy and I kept each other company, going up to the club for meals together, washing on the roof, and accepting joint invitations out to dinner in the evenings, when Maisy, sadly conscious of her unglamorous appearance in slacks and bedroom slippers, would produce a pocketbook photograph of herself to show what she could look like when given a fair change.

'Wouldn't think that was me, would you?' she would say, with a mixture of pride and pathos.

* * *

When, a few days later, we heard that the *Marnix* had gone down while being towed to land seven miles from the shore, Maisy confided to me, somewhat disarmingly, that all the pretty nighties she had brought to help 'cheer up the boys' must now be at the bottom of the sea.

We saw the OC Troops for a few minutes at dinner one night in the café and he told us more about the shipwreck, about how the *Marnix* had kept afloat and most of the troops had stayed on its decks all night and about how nearly everybody had been rescued. The only fatal casualties had been one Dutchman who had gone mad and jumped overboard and one man whom 'we had to shoot', said the OC, with a pained look coming across his kindly face. The man had been caught looting from the first-class cabins. The OC himself had stayed on board. None of them had had anything to eat, save for the Javanese who killed a tame rabbit and devoured it raw. He praised the troops from the decks below who had filed out in perfect order when the explosion occurred, although they knew that those at the back, anyway, would not have stood an earthly chance if the ship had sunk quickly.

Other shiploads of survivors kept on arriving throughout the week and fresh batches of officers from camps further up the coast would come to town each day. There were relieved, joyful meetings from which a whole new crop of engagements would result. Of these, among the women I knew, three out of four engagements were broken off during the following couple of months.

* * *

We had all been provided with toothbrushes, combs and soap the day after the shipwreck and then, after a while, a great bundle of army vests, pants and battle dresses arrived to be sorted out and tried on amid laughter mingled with dismay. The garments felt horribly coarse and rough against the skin and of course nothing fitted.

Then Maisy and I went out to lunch with a colonel and a major who were just leaving for England. Maisy was hitting it off with the major, while the colonel bored me with a continuous stream of feeble dirty stories throughout luncheon, tea and dinner. Being unable to get Maisy away from the major, I just had to stick it out until the colonel, finally realizing that he was not getting anywhere, suddenly changed tack and became fatherly, promising to telephone my mother when he got back to England to tell her that he had seen me safe and well. Since he also presented me with a warm camel-hair dressing gown, Aertex underwear, soft drill shirts and trousers that were so much pleasanter to wear than the army stuff, I was really grateful to him, though all the same not sorry that his boat was leaving the next day. My husband wore the dressing gown for many years.

* * *

Then the wonderful news arrived that we were to be taken to Tunis in army lorries on the following Sunday and from there were to be flown to Cairo. But the next day we heard that this was all off, that we might be staying on in North Africa indefinitely and that we were going to be banded together into a show entitled the 'ENSA vivors'.

That night, a Friday, I stayed in the hostel feeling too fed up and miserable to want to go anywhere while Maisy and little Roberta went to the casino along the coast road. I turned one pair of the colonel's trousers into a skirt, with inverted pleats back and front, and ate up my 'emergency ration' chocolate, taking great pleasure in defying the notice on the outside of the tin that said it was 'only to be opened under orders from a superior officer'. But the atmosphere of the place was so horribly depressing that I felt I could not bear to stay in again.

* * *

The following morning news came once more that we would be leaving and this time it would definitely be at six o'clock the next morning. A heavy load seemed to be lifted off my spirits and that night Maisy, Roberta and I hitchhiked to the casino. The army major, who ran the establishment, had fallen madly in love with Maisy — she seemed to have rather a lot of success with majors — and had arranged a little party.

The casino, which was situated almost on the beach and which had a sunroof and wide verandas, could have been an attractive place, but it was very dilapidated. The dusty stone dance floor was crowded with soldiers, a few of them were from the *Marnix* but the majority were men stationed in the permanent camp. There were only a handful of women to go round, nurses from the hospital and us from ENSA. Some of the men had been at the camp for two or three years and the nurses were the only English women they ever saw. It was obvious how few they met from the wolfish way in which they looked at us and because in the 'excuse me' dance they were like a lot of dogs fighting over a few bones.

Outside the main entrance, after the dancing was over, the leader of a group of young sex-starved officers, who probably had not managed to get a single dance that evening, asked me in a tone of almost desperate pathos: 'please kiss us goodnight, Miss, please kiss us goodnight.' I am afraid I just could not face doing the round of them all and looked hastily about for Maisy, but she was upstairs on the roof with the major sobbing over her — 'most embarrassing, my dears, I didn't know what to do,' she told us afterwards.

That night, when we returned to the hostel I had violent pains and was very sick. I thought with horror that if I were really ill I might not be able to go with the others in the morning. But the idea of being left behind, even in a clean hospital, was not to be thought of and I decided to say nothing and get up and go with the rest, whatever I felt like in the morning.

6

To Tunis by Lorry: An Uncomfortable Journey

We were called at an early hour before it was yet light and bundled our few possessions into army kitbags. Then everyone, except me, went up to the officers' club for breakfast. I sat on my kitbag in one of the dirty passages of the hostel waiting for them to come back and thinking with joy that this was the last half hour in this godforsaken place, and soon we would be putting miles between Phillipville and us. I was still feeling ghastly, but this did not worry me much.

When everyone had arrived back, we climbed into the lorries waiting outside in the still dark and quiet street. Maisy, who was being kindness itself towards me, wanted me to come in the lorry with the rest of her party so that she could 'look after' me, but I had to go with the rest of the 'pool'. They wisely let me have a seat next to the opening at the back. Our departure was held up for about half an hour because one of the women was missing — tall and beautiful Joan, who had found herself a room somewhere else in the town with a couple of French Ats, also off the *Marnix*, was still fast asleep in bed. Fortunately, someone knew where they were staying or we might have been kept waiting indefinitely.

The journey that day is hardly one of my happiest

memories, travelling as we were from six o'clock in the morning until eight o'clock at night, sitting on wooden seats in big lumbering army lorries bumping along the roughest of roads. It was enough to make one feel sick without a severe bilious attack on top of it all.

But we were on the move at last; anything could be endured and how exciting it was to think that we would be sleeping that night in Tunis, which had figured so large in the recent war news.

What a magnificent sunrise it was that morning. The sky was a flaming red, suffusing the whole countryside with a deep ruby glow, the outlines of the hills standing out sharp and clean-cut in the clear morning air.

We travelled across the plains for quite a while before the road started winding up into the hills. I am afraid I cannot describe the scenery on this trip very accurately because I felt better when I had my eyes shut and so I kept them closed most of the time, but I had to open them to look out sometimes at the wonderful views we were then passing as the road wound higher and higher and all around us were wild and desolate hills, with rich green valleys between. How wasteful it seemed to pass such miles upon miles of quite isolated and yet fertile-looking land, while the English countryside is so fast being eaten away by spreading towns. Here, there were acres upon acres to spare.

We stopped for lunch at a wayside hotel where I had a glass of brandy to keep me going; we then went straight back into the lorries and on again in an attempt to reach Tunis before nightfall. We wound down to the plains again and the sun went down when we still had quite a few miles to go.

It was dark when we eventually drove through the streets of the town, but everybody immediately became wide awake and looked about with pleasure at the sight of a large town with civilized streets and pavements. For me, it seemed to evoke the flavour of Paris; it had the same type of trams;

there were trees down the centre of the main boulevard; the advertisements and shops signs were all written in French but, most of all, its smell was surprisingly and deliciously Parisienne.

* * *

What a joy it was to arrive at a scrupulously clean hostel, to slip between fresh white sheets and there to sleep long and deeply. The hostel was a little way out from the centre of the town. It was a simple stone-floored house with orange trees growing between the flagged paving stones. The woman in charge of the hostel was English; she was kind and fussy, and soon put my tummy right.

There was also a Jewish male servant, Joseph, who told us all, time and time again while we were there, the story of how the Germans had taken his son away to work, of how his son had escaped and come home again and of how he, his father, had put him to bed and when the German police arrived to fetch him he told them that he was ill and that he, Joseph, would take his place. He illustrated his story with dramatic gestures, which were identical for each telling. Joseph would let his enormous head repose on his hands and look soulful when describing the boy asleep; he would bang 'knock, knock' on a handy piece of furniture and look threatening when describing the Germans' arrival and, finally, there would be great strikings of the breast when Joseph offered his services in place of his son's.

* * *

The morning after our arrival, we got up late and then decided to take a trip into town to have a look at the shops. We were, however, very disappointed because there was little more to buy here than there had been in Phillipville. I do, however, remember seeing a beautiful chiffon nightie priced at an outrageously high sum displayed all by itself in a shop window.

That morning, those who had been chosen for the first group to leave by plane, which included the Rhythm Sisters, were taken to the RAF airport to be ready in case there was a vacancy on a plane leaving for Cairo. However, they arrived back at lunchtime to report 'no go'. The same thing happened on the two following mornings. Then a terrible rumour circulated that there would never be room on the planes for us all to travel by air and that we were to be taken back to Phillipville by army lorry and there, with all the other ENSA people who had remained at Constantine and Bone, be put on a ship to complete the journey by sea. This certainly was a bitter blow.

* * *

That evening, Pamela told a few of us, including Maisy, Belle, the red-haired crooner from the band show and me that they had met some American pilots at the airport who had invited Anita, Clare and herself to their seaside bungalow that night. They had also asked them to invite a few friends to make up the party. Pamela told us that they were all 'grand fun' and that with a bit of persuasion might manage to arrange for us to fly to Cairo from their own airport, for the Americans had far fewer rules and regulations than the RAF.

So, when they arrived in jeeps at about seven o'clock, we were all waiting expectantly. Maisy and I got into the back of one jeep together, but this course of action was not allowed. Some tough guy demanded, 'here, what sort of a party is this?' and made Maisy join him in the front, while his friend George climbed in beside me.

The ten-mile drive to their bungalow was taken at breakneck speed, with the jeeps racing each other along the airport road. However, we eventually arrived and piled out of the jeeps, shaken but undaunted. Anita had not come with us because Charles, who had managed to come on with her, was in Tunis.

Inside the bungalow, we were first taken up to the bar and offered drinks; I said I would have a gin and lime. The usual British manner of pouring this drink is of course to put an inch of gin at the bottom of a small glass and then to add a suitable quantity of lime, but these American airmen merely slopped a whole lot of spirit into a tumbler, so that when the lime was added the glass brimmed over. It was no wonder that my head was reeling before I was half way through it. In fact, reeling heads were the order of the day: we danced a bit to the radio, but it was always 'back to the bar, back to the bar'.

Later on in the evening, heavy-faced George, my partner, suggested a variation: 'Waddya say to a spot of dinner?' Personally I did not say 'no', and so Belle, Maisy and I, with George and two others, tore into town again in a couple of the jeeps, leaving the rest to go on getting drunk while Pamela, as stolid as ever, stood behind the bar, back at her old barmaid's job of mixing cocktails.

With dinner at a cafe, which I quite enjoyed, being over, we tore back to the orgy. This time I got together with Pamela and Clare, who had been making chicken sandwiches for themselves in the kitchen, to start pumping our hosts about the possibilities of vacancies on American planes flying to Cairo.

'We'll fix you', they said, 'Shure, we'll take you yourselves. You be up at the airport, sheven o'clock tomorrow morning — shorry thish morning.' They were so drunk by this time that we really did not know whether to take them at their word or not, but that was all we could get out of them — 'Shure, we'll fix you.' One young pilot came staggering out of a bedroom with a loaded revolver, which he started to fire, fortunately out of the window onto the beach.

Most of us began to feel that it was about time to go and

prevailed upon the soberest of the party, who had arrived late, to drive us back to town.

I suppose that it was between two and three o'clock when we reached the hostel and Pamela, Maisy, Clare and I began a long argument over whether we should try to get to the aerodrome by seven or whether it would be no earthly use because the Americans could not have been serious. I was all in favour of getting up and going out there at any rate. We could only lose our night's sleep and might be in Cairo by the next day.

'How on earth will we get all the way out there?' Maisy wanted to know. She thought it would be a waste of time. I said we would have to hitchhike.

So we decided to go to bed for a couple of hours' sleep, relying on Clare, who was herself keen to go and was good at waking up, to call us at five o'clock. Someone would have to go to the other part of the hostel building to wake Anita, who was sleeping over there.

'And she'll never be ready in time,' said Pamela. Anita had been late for breakfast every morning while on board the *Marnix*.

7

To Cairo by Air: Pilots Commandeer a Plane

A t five o'clock punctually, Clare came and turned us out of bed. I think we all felt that we were embarking on a wild goose chase, but there was excitement in the air nevertheless. We rose and dressed as silently as possible, not wishing anybody in authority — either the woman who ran the hostel or one the company managers — to know what we were up to, for they might have stopped us leaving.

Maisy, with whom I was sharing a room, remained in bed while I dressed and put my things into my kitbag; when I tried to wake her she only grunted, so I concluded that she had thought better of going. However, before leaving the room I gave her a 'goodbye' kiss on the forehead, which made her wake up with a start and announce that of course she was coming too. Clare and Pamela were not yet ready, so I myself slipped over to wake Anita. She was thrilled to hear of the possibility of a plane and got up at once. I carried over a heap of things for her to pack in her kitbag, which was with her sister's and Pamela's in their room.

It was not long before Anita came over. It was by now half past five and I felt sure that we ought to be going, for we did not know how long it would take us to hitchhike the ten miles out to the aerodrome. The others, however, were busy making up their faces and arranging their hair just so, and took no notice of my entreaties to hurry up and let their faces go. In fact they got as exasperated with me as I was getting with them and told me to 'shut up'.

At long last they were ready and we started to creep down the stairs with our kitbags, feeling rather like schoolgirls sneaking off on a midnight picnic.

Suddenly Joseph appeared in the hall. We hushed him into silence, let him help us with our bags, then tipped him as well as we could and wished him an affectionate goodbye outside in the street. It was not far to lug our bags to the corner, from where the road to the airport branched off, so when we got there we dropped them down and waited.

* * *

The minutes went by and the sky became lighter and lighter, but no vehicle passed in the direction in which we wanted to go. We were beginning to look quite hopelessly at each other when suddenly a decrepit-looking taxi came creaking down the main street.

We dropped our bags and rushed at it, shrieking at the tops of our voices. The man pulled up and we got in, the five of us filling it completely, so more precious minutes were lost while the kitbags were tied on the back and up on the roof. Still, it was only about twenty minutes to seven when we reached the airport. The taxi driver of course wanted to charge the earth, but we managed to beat him down a bit — we did not have enough money to pay him what he had asked for anyhow.

Pamela and Clare went off to enquire whether our friends had arrived yet, while the rest of us sat on a seat outside to keep watch for when they should turn up. Once more the minutes ticked by, while our spirits began to droop again, especially when Pamela returned to report that they were not yet on the 'drome' and seven o'clock came and went.

* * *

Ten minutes later George and Clarence, looking amazingly self-possessed and sober after the condition in which we had left them not so very many hours previously, came bounding up the drive in a jeep. They were taken aback at seeing us, never having expected that we would really get up and come out there on our own, but they reassured us that all would be well and that they would see us off to Cairo then and there. When we saw the size of the aeroplane, a 30-seater transporter, we felt that it would be a shame for the rest of them back at the hostel not to come too, so Pamela and Maisy asked to be driven back to town to collect them and to return with them as speedily as possible.

Meanwhile, Anita, Clare and I were taken off to be given breakfast in a shed. It seemed a long time before the others came back with the other members of the 'pool'; there was insufficient room for the other two companies to come too. Considering that everybody had to be collected from more than one place, that they had to get out of bed and pack their things and that it was a ten-mile drive either way in and out of town, they were really remarkably quick. Then, to top it all, there had been a fight with the proprietress of the hostel who had not wanted to let them go because it was unofficial and she had had no orders from ENSA. But with a vision before their eyes of another army lorry journey back to Phillipville, followed by a return to the ocean waves, everyone turned a deaf ear to her protests.

* * *

When everyone arrived at the aerodrome, there was an attempt to put things on a more official footing. With Bobby having discovered that his girlfriend was working in a show in the vicinity and so wishing to remain behind, Big David was now 'pool manager' and he took it upon himself to take and list everyone's name. We rather resented the way in which Big David rather dictatorially asked us for our names when, after all, it was we who had arranged the whole thing. It removed some of the gilt off the gingerbread of the adventure, though perhaps a touch of officialdom was just as well, for previously the pilot and our friends, who were of course coming too, had been talking of stopping for the night in Tripoli and winking at one another. However, we eventually all climbed into the plane, sat down on seats facing the centre and fastened our seatbelts for takeoff.

* * *

Though I had always had rather a horror of aeroplanes, a fear my mother had planted in me as a child, I now felt that I would rather go in anything other than another ship and was not in the least nervous, only excited, when we began to tear along the runway gathering speed with a terrific acceleration and then let go from the earth and soar into the air.

It was a beautiful day. As we had started far too late in the morning to have any hope of reaching Cairo that night, the pilot, a young man with eyes as bright a blue as the sky beneath which he was flying, did not hurry but followed the coastline so that we could look down from the window at the crinkled sea on one side and the sun-drenched land on the other. The toy houses, villages and farms below belonged to a world from which we were quite remote and I felt no fear at being so far from an earth with which I felt I had ceased to have any connection.

Later, we began to pass over the Libyan Desert: desolate and lifeless it lay below, slimy green and grey with oily rivers crawling to the sea.

It was late afternoon and eight hours from the time we first took off when the pilot circled Tripoli aerodrome and brought us down with hardly a bump.

* * *

Tripoli airport is about twenty miles out of the town and we had to wait a while for a conveyance to arrive to take us in. The country we went through on the way was flat, dried up and uninteresting except for the camels we passed on the road, but Tripoli itself struck me as having been a fine town before the war had knocked it about. We passed some beautiful buildings of Italian architecture and the hotel where it had been arranged for us to spend the night was built to a lovely design. Courtyards with gardens and fountains open to the sky were laid out round the main halls, while cloister-like passages ran round the courtyards and the rooms opened onto these. I could not understand why one had to go down a staircase and along a subterranean passage to get to the dining room, but next morning at breakfast, when the window shutters were drawn, I saw the point. The dining room had been built across the other side of the road from the main building, so it was right down by the harbour with a wonderful view out over the sea from three sides of the room. It was like having breakfast on board ship.

This magnificent hotel, however, was not much better off than the officers' club at Phillipville had been for such things as cutlery and glasses, so we still had to drink out of the lower halves of bottles.

A half Italian half American friend of mine in England had said that if I ever went to Tripoli on my travels I was to be sure to look up her relatives there. So, forgetting Italy's only very recent participation in the war, I tried to reach Admiral Fienzi on the telephone, but only managed to get hold of the military police.

The next morning was cloudy and wet and we did not leave as early as had originally been intended, the idea being to reach Cairo before darkness fell. Clarence and George took turns at the controls.

* * *

I do not think that any of us enjoyed the first part of the flight that day. We were surrounded by clouds, could see nothing and it was horribly bumpy and, though nobody said anything, I could tell from looking at their faces that they disliked the experience as much as I did.

At midday, however, we left the rain clouds behind and the sun began to stream down on the parched thirsty-looking desert below; the bumping came to an end and we all relaxed.

Eagerly, we started looking out for the ruins of tanks and armoured cars left behind after Montgomery's great rout of the German army.

* * *

At El Adam, we came down to fill the aeroplane up with petrol, and us up with tea, but this was made with such salty water that we really felt thirstier after we had drunk it than before. But it was a wonderful experience to be having it in the middle of the Western Desert, with nothing but sand stretching in all directions. From photographs I had previously seen of the desert I had been unable to understand how some writers could possibly have felt such a fascination for it, but I now realized that it was the vivid sunlight and contrasting shadows on the rolling sands that gave it that strange magnetic beauty. It is monotonous, unsympathetic but wonderful in the sun; in the moonlight it is unforgettable.

We were hurried through our tea while the plane was being filled with petrol and then speedily took off again, leaving El Adam miles behind. Long before we reached Cairo, however, the dusk closed in and darkness shut off the earth.

* * *

It was glorious flying through the night. The wing of the aeroplane stretched out from below the window at which I was sitting and I thought how lovely it would be to dance along it to where a star seemed to twinkle at the other end.

We were told that we would be coming down in half an hour and everyone twisted round in his or her seats to look down for the first sight of Cairo. Then, stretching out far away beneath us a mass of glittering lights came into view, breathtakingly beautiful, as if approaching a magical city in a fairy tale.

And now that we were right over the aerodrome, search-lights came shooting out to guide us in. The plane banked over, the world tipped up at us, we circled round the gleaming track of runway that was coming nearer and nearer until we met it and ran along it, smoothly and easily, until we came to a gentle halt.

We were in Cairo at last.

8

Arrival in Cairo: Reunion and Marriage

S ince that first arrival by aeroplane I have returned to Cairo three times — by sea from India via Suez and a short train journey; by road from Palestine; and by train down from Syria — and each time has had echoes of the magical thrill of that first arrival. Of course, apart from the first time when I was arriving to meet him, I was always returning to my husband, and since places and people become so closely identified with each other it is virtually impossible to separate one's feelings from one's impressions.

For me, Cairo was a city that throbbed with vitality and that glowed and sparkled with light. I found the brilliant sunshine by day and the mass of illuminations by night intoxicating to my blackout weary eyes. It was a city of contrasts; one could travel from the traffic-crowded streets and smart shops in the centre of the town, out over the Nile where the houses of the wealthy stood along its banks to the play gardens of green Gezira island, back again and down side streets where poverty and dirt were blatantly exposed on every side. Then there was the Mousky bazaar where stores displaying brilliantly-coloured silks, brasswear, jewellery and oriental perfumes lined the narrow streets and alleys and where you jostled among Arabs in black flowing robes, among heavily veiled women, bare-footed urchins, flocks of sheep and even an occasional stray donkey. Emerging from the dust and bustle of the Mousky you came upon mosques, stately and beautiful, wonderfully carved old Arabic houses and, rising above them, the citadel with its dome and slender minarets crowning the city from the hilltop.

From there one had a marvellous view over the town and beyond to the smoothly-flowing blue Nile and open emerald green, flat, palm-studded country to where the pyramids rose up on the horizon. I have always thought that the pyramids were most spectacular when seen from some way off, when they formed part of the landscape, as in ancient Egyptian drawings. On the horizon, they dominate the view and add to its pictorial and stylized beauty.

Looking down from the citadel walls one can see over the dead city, hushed and weird, with ruined cemeteries and mosques, and mountains of desolate grey sand. Behind lie the distant hills, dried up and barren.

* * *

The atmosphere of Cairo caught me in its grip straightaway on that first evening as we drove through the streets from the aerodrome: the mix of the crowds on the pavements with the *fellahin* in his flapping *gallabiyeh* and the wealthy fat Egyptian in a European suit and crimson *tarbush* rubbing shoulders with British Tommies, American GIs, Greeks, Armenians, Poles and Slovaks. There was the thrill of the brightly lit shop windows, of fruit stores in which oranges and bananas hung thickly and invitingly — 'I only joined ENSA to eat a banana again,' remarked Pamela — and of the fashionable and brilliantly lit shops in the centre of the town. It seemed extraordinary to see so many cars on the streets again. Taxis, which were hardly to be procured for love or money in the London we had left behind, were here gliding past the whole time touting for customers.

Ragged little boys in dirty 'nightshirts' would go tearing after them in the hope of opening a door for a prospective traveller and so earn a piastre or two. Trams would come along the centre of the road, a mass of swarming *tarbush*ed humanity clinging on wherever it was possible to get a hold.

The beggars were a depressing sight. Women in the black dresses and veils the lower classes in Egypt always wear would hold out half starved little miseries of children — I learnt afterwards that a lot of these children are hired out for begging purposes — and cripples would thrust out their withered limbs from squatting positions on the pavement's edge.

We turned into Opera Square, which was brighter than ever with lights. A roof garden restaurant built in tiers and dazzlingly illuminated caught my fancy, and I thought how lovely it would be to be having dinner at one of those tables overlooking the square, open to the night sky.

* * *

We turned off into another street to call at the ENSA general headquarters' office to find out where we were to stay. Big David had rung up previously from the airport to announce our arrival and now he went upstairs to the office, leaving the rest of us outside in the bus.

'Please ask if there are any letters,' I reminded him. However, he forgot, and excused himself, saying curtly, 'Who on earth could want letters at a time like this?' I actually wanted nothing else, but did not say so.

David had come back with one of the ENSA staff officers and a woman in uniform who was in charge of billeting. Some of the company were dropped off at the Metropolitan Hotel, but most of us were dropped at the National.

I was so sick of living in close proximity with other people that I asked the manager if I might have a single room. He said he had a small one, which was a 'very nice room' with a 'very nice bath'. When I got upstairs I found that it was in fact a bathroom with a bed put up in it. The hotel was certainly very overcrowded at the time and officers were sleeping three or four to a room. I was so thankful to be on my own that I raised no objection to my bathroom, though it was trying having always to remember to keep the door locked because otherwise a breezy looming gentleman, towel slung over the shoulder and shaving things in one hand, would come bursting in to beat an embarrassed retreat the next minute.

We had dinner in a large saloon, where dark-skinned waiters in white *gallabiyeh*s, turbans and scarlet sashes rustled between the tables bearing dishes. Then I went upstairs, so sleepy that I wonder I did not take my bath in the bed and sleep in the bath.

* * *

Next morning we were all taken off to the offices. In Cairo at that time ENSA had three separate offices in different parts of the town and a year later there were four. The one in Kasr el Nil was for administration and all official business and it was there, on the second floor, that one posted one's letters. One collected letters, on the other hand, in Shara Borza, a back street that was difficult to find. You also went there for billeting enquiries or complaints, or to report 'sick' — if you could walk that far.

For rehearsals we had to go to Zulfigar, which was near Abdin Palace. We also had to go there (though much later on) to be measured in the wardrobe and, most important of all, to get paid.

That morning we started off by sitting in the administration office signing fresh papers with which to acquire our British identity cards, with a double dose of signing for those whose passports had gone down with the *Marnix*. I managed to slip upstairs for a chat with the kind and helpful post corporal about sending off two important cables, one to England and one to Syria. Later on in the day he himself took me round to Marconi House.

* * *

Once the signing had been completed, we were taken over to Zulfigar where we each had a little talk with a Mr Mann about what costumes we would need to have made before we could start working in a show. I decided to ask for a Mexican and a waltz dress, which would be suitable for two numbers in which I would not have to dance *en pointe*. I had actually saved a couple of pairs of pointe shoes in my 'panic bag', but I could not tell how long it would be before I got a new supply sent out from England, so thought it safer not to rely on just two pairs because they wear out so quickly.

In the accounts department, a smooth-faced and pleasant Captain Nightingale told us that of course we would all get our insurance money paid in due course and in the meanwhile we were to be advanced £50 each for our immediate needs.

* * *

It was fun to have £50 in one's purse and to be surrounded by tempting shops full of uncouponed goods, but when it means starting absolutely from scratch, £50 does not go very far in a place as expensive as Cairo was in 1943. Owing to a very economical upbringing, I think I made my money go further than most of the others did, but when it was all spent there was still a mass of things I wanted but was unable to buy.

Most women find it exciting to buy new clothes and I was no exception. Having come from wartime London, where any sense of fashion was virtually non-existent, we were delighted by the stylish frocks in Cairo's shops and most of all by the handbags and shoes.

But eventually we all discovered the same thing; though the garments, shoes and bags looked very attractive when they were new, the workmanship on them was very poor and slipshod. So long as the garment looked good enough in the shop window, the general attitude was one of *malesh*. *Malesh*, which means 'it doesn't matter' or 'we couldn't care less', is one of the Egyptians' favourite words. The seams of dresses would come undone, fasteners would fall off handbags in no time and I have never known a Cairo zip to work more than twice before breaking.

* * *

For the first week we chiefly spent our days shopping and in the evenings officers staying in the hotel would invite us out to openair cinemas and cabarets.

I saw some good films that week, but disliked being bitten by bugs every time I went out, which even in the very best cinemas seemed inevitable. There were no continuous performances; the last showing used to start at 9.30 p.m. and there was always an interval at 10.00 p.m. during which the radio news would be broadcast before the main picture came on. I always enjoyed listening to Egypt's chirpy national anthem at the end of the programme. The British soldiers in Egypt concocted a parody of it, which I am unable to quote here because every soldier I have ever known has been too modest to repeat it. A major I once met told me that he had first heard the soldiers' version sung while he was in hospital and, not realizing that it was to the tune of the national anthem, when he heard the anthem played at an important function he burst out laughing, to everyone's embarrassment.

Most of the cabarets in Cairo consisted chiefly of dancing and it was very feeble dancing at that. The Egyptian women did their belly dance of course, but the only pleasing aspect I saw in it was its spontaneity. The women wriggled happily on and on, with the music following them until it seemed as if they had grown bored with the routine and so stopped. There were also dancers of various European nationalities, but the only ones who made any real impression on me were a couple of Spaniards, a man and a woman, who were brilliant. They were encored uproariously every night at the Ambassadors, and richly deserved all the applause they got. The man, the finer dancer of the two, possessed a body that was as taut and as flexible as sprung steel, and the fire of the dance ran through him to his fingertips. I saw some excellent acrobats too that week at the Bardia cabaret, where I must not forget to mention old Madam Bardia, who still made an unconquerable appearance, leading her troop at the age of 60.

* * *

I saw very little of Maisy and the Rhythm Sisters that week. I had grown quite fond of them after all we had been through together, but we had too little in common for any continued friendship.

Indeed, in the daytime when I was not on my own I found myself mostly going about with a young woman called Veda who played an accordion with her sister Peggy. Both Peggy and Veda had become engaged at Phillipville, Peggy to an RAF officer, Veda to the handsome Dutch steward who used to survey the scene at meal times on board ship, but both engagements fizzled out very quickly.

* * *

At the end of the week, the ENSA billeting woman said that I was to move to the Metropolitan Hotel. I did not want to go, although everyone said that it was much nicer there than at the National, but they had now given me a proper room on my own and at the Metropolitan I would have to share again with Pamela, who did not want to leave her single room at the National either. But we both had to go and, after grunting at each other for a bit at first, settled down and decided that the Metropolitan was really very nice and that it was most convenient to have a private bathroom between us, and we got on as well together as we had done on board the *Marnix*.

Pamela was already bored with Cairo. Even the bananas had lost their attraction, along with the oranges and Groppi cream cakes. She told me that she had seen all the nightlife Cairo had to offer. She had been to the Gezira sporting club and had gone to, seen and been disillusioned by the pyramids. What else was there to do? She wanted to start working, for she had never been so poor in her life before.

In fact, everyone soon became impatient with sitting around in the Metropolitan Hotel doing nothing, but they all had to wait until new costumes could be made and shows organized. The company we had parted from in Tunis arrived at about this time by air and, being a band show, they told us gloomily that they would have to wait a long time before they could start working because new instruments were having to be sent out from England.

* * *

Stage people always dislike prolonged holidays, partly because they are usually over-brimming with energy, partly because so few of them have any interest in anything outside their own profession, but chiefly I think because of the way the stage gets into their blood and gives them no peace.

It was Christmas before a show made up of 'pool' artists and put together by Mr Paine was ready to set out for the Canal Zone. Up until then everybody continued to sit around the Metropolitan Hotel with gloomy faces; and those who were not in this show went on sitting around for even longer.

I believe I was the only one who did not care how long it took before we started to work again because at that time I was living in a world apart, meeting my husband, getting married and going off on our honeymoon to an oasis up the Nile.

9

As Principal Dancer with
the *Fol de Rols*

A few days before Christmas my husband's leave came to an end and he had to return to his section in Syria, which he had left three weeks previously. I felt desperately lonely and quite out of touch with the ENSA crowd at the Metropolitan Hotel.

* * *

For Christmas day I had received a luncheon invitation from a Bedouin Arab friend of my husband's called Tahar el Araby. Tahar had recently finished serving a 20-year prison sentence for having in his youth got himself involved in a plot to assassinate the British field marshal Herbert Kitchener. Now, however, he was a mild, humorous and intensely pro-British old man; his walls were thick with photographs of Winston Churchill and of the royal family and he was engaged in secret service work for the British.

Tahar had invited six Egyptian friends, all of whom were male, six British Tommies and me. In accordance with Bedouin custom, Tahar's wife would never sit down to a meal with her husband's guests — she merely served the food and then withdrew — so it fell upon me to try and get the silent smiling Egyptians to talk and the British soldiers, who were eyeing the really delicious Arabic food as if it were the cat's dinner, to eat something. I myself loved the Arabic dishes, which ranged from minced meat and rice rolled tightly in vine leaves to really delicious sweetmeats: my favourite, which looked like a haystack dripping in honey, virtually melted in one's mouth.

* * *

I was not sorry when, after Christmas was over, Ivan Campbell, one of the ENSA producers, who had travelled out with us on the *Marnix* and was now in Cairo, told me that I should soon start rehearsing with the *Fol de Rols*.

All I had done up until then was to take part in a variety programme that Stainless Stephen had put on for three nights in which Avril Angers had featured.

The *Fol de Rols* had been going for years as a popular summer show in England and the members of this latest company were arriving on the next convoy from England. Mr Campbell wanted to know if my new costumes and my music were nearly ready, for the music for my dances had gone down with the *Marnix*.

I had to go down to the music section one day and hum through my Mexican number, while a sergeant on the ENSA musical staff took it down. I have always had great difficulty singing in tune, so this was rather an ordeal. The sergeant was extraordinarily quick at interpreting what I was trying to sing, jotting it down and helping put me back on the right note every time I wandered off it, but it must have been a trial for him too and he had my full sympathy. I felt no offence when the female secretary asked politely, but with an anxious look, 'You don't sing by any chance do you?' I assured her that I only danced.

* * *

I was feeling horribly out of practice and, with the thought of starting work again, began to make enquiries about ballet schools in Cairo.

I was told of one school, which I went to see, which was run by an Americanized Romanian with scarlet hair. She told me that she had no professional pupils, but I stayed on to watch a class of very young girls. Music was supplied by a gramophone, but heaven knows why they took the trouble to wind the thing up, as Madame set the steps regardless of what music was being played and her pupils danced, or rather stumbled about, equally regardless.

* * *

I felt I could practise better on my own and later was introduced to a Viennese teacher of central European dancing who very kindly let me come and work in her studio when she herself was not teaching.

She was a charming little woman, overflowing with enthusiasm that was being wasted on her Egyptian pupils whom, she told me, were lazy and easily satisfied with themselves, convinced that they had nothing more to learn and were star performers after two terms.

* * *

By this time a further party of wrecked ENSA employees, comprising several shows, had arrived in Cairo, still in their battledress. They had certainly had a worse time than we had had with our aeroplane hitchhike. They, poor wretches, had been put onto another ship at Phillipville with a lot of soldiers and officers from the *Marnix* who were continuing their journey on to India. It had been a small ship and they had been so overcrowded on board that heaven knows how many of them could have been saved if anything had happened. Everyone knew that there were not nearly enough boats and rafts to go round.

They were attacked twice before reaching Alexandria and then during the train journey down to Cairo the train was derailed. It was fortunately not a bad accident, but just a final little thrill for them.

A little later on another accident happened to an ENSA party, which included Anita, Clare and Pamela. They were being driven back from a performance in the Canal Zone when the bus they were in skidded off the roadside and turned over completely. By a miracle, very few people were badly hurt, save for one young woman who had her fingers crushed and, given that she was an acrobat, would never be able to work again. They all got covered in broken glass though and arrived back in Cairo badly shaken. I remember how one young woman who was seemingly quite all right suddenly burst into tears and then fainted in the hall of the Metropolitan Hotel. Pamela announced to me privately that she had 'had' ENSA now.

* * *

The day came for my first rehearsal with the *Fol de Rols* and I went down to Zulfigar Palace wondering what the company would be like.

It consisted of four elderly gentlemen, each white-haired and portly, whom I immediately privately christened the 'teddy bears'. One of the teddy bears, Harry, was the leading comedian and an excellent one he was too with his own brand of simple down-to-earth clean humour. A second teddy bear, Gregg, was manager of the party. Naturally, there were no young men in the show. There were four young women, all attractive and good dancers, and Gladys, a very nice-looking soprano singer with whom I became quite friendly for the short time I was with the show. I might have become more so, but friendships are continually being broken up in stage life. To complete the party, there was sandy-haired Scott, who compèred the show and also did his own cigarette act, and two pianists, Sydney and Kathleen, husband and wife and both first-class players who gave the show a great lift. Finally, there was Renée, who had been invited to join the company for a few weeks as a guest artist.

Renée was the wife of a well-known English comedian with whom she had appeared in many London productions. On hearing that she was with us I immediately became interested, for I had never seen her on stage before and looked forward to seeing her perform. She struck me at first as being very pleasant; she did not give herself airs and graces and was friendly and natural with the young women in the show.

Later on, when I witnessed her violent dislike of Gladys, which she showed quite plainly, I became aware of the extent of her passion and fierce pride and tried to steer clear of her.

Afterwards, however, when we had both left the *Fol de Rols* and joined another company and I came to know her better and understand her many-sided nature, I became very fond of her. She was temperamental to a degree and as sensitive as stage artists usually are who have not allowed themselves to become so hard-boiled that they virtually cease to be artists.

Renée was definitely neither conceited nor expected to be treated like a star, for she mucked in with everybody in the dressing rooms and was friendly to all alike. If, however, she suspected anyone of not respecting her position or of slighting her in any way, then there was the devil to pay.

Renée was a real trooper. Strong as a horse, she would never miss a performance and would sometimes carry on at a mess party after the show until five or six in the morning, drinking everyone else flat on the floor. She was popular everywhere she went and, with her great gift for entertaining, fund of stories and superb sense of humour, she was usually the life and soul of the party.

* * *

To return to the *Fol de Rols*, Ivan Campbell, also white-haired and elderly but not stout enough to be classed a 'teddy bear', took the rehearsals. He was a kindly man who knew his job inside out.

The first day we went through the opening,

'Hello, pleased to meet you;

We are the *Fol de Rols*;

May we say, "How d'you do?"'

This was real concert-party stuff.

Then Mr Campbell took me aside to tell me in which numbers he wanted me to appear as principal dancer.

First there was *Daffodils* in which Gladys sang the refrain; the four young women danced and I had to arrange a solo for myself after seeing what patterns their steps made, so that I could harmonize mine in the foreground with theirs in the background and noting when they left the stage for me to 'take it alone'.

For this number we wore long floating transparent dresses — the others' yellow, mine green. I decided to do my part on pointe until my two pairs of shoes wore out, hoping that replacements would arrive before my toes wore out along with the shoes. In nearly every ENSA show there was a number of this type — 'someone singing and young things flitting', as my husband described them.

* * *

I was also to appear in the tiny part of an usherette in a cinema sketch called *The Pedlar* in which Harry and Renée played two deaf members of the audience misunderstanding each other. Then, besides my own solo, the Mexican dance, I had to do a little 'bit' in the Scotch finale in front of the four women, all in Highland kilts. They had two numbers on their own in the show, a duelling dance, and 'half and half', in which they were dressed so that one side of each of them resembled a girl, the other a soldier boy. The dancers in Act Four were good and they did their number slickly and well.

Renée called her spot *Goodbye*. In it, she presented an assortment of character studies of the various types of goodbyes. It was a clever number but too subtle for a good many of our troop audiences, who found the broadness of Harry's humour far easier to appreciate.

A good little sketch, which always went down with a bang at the end of the programme, was *Christmas Eve*, a parody of old-time melodrama in which Harry played an unruly member of an audience in a box at one side of the stage who created interruptions throughout the performance.

* * *

I have not yet mentioned our sergeant stage manager Busty, but he was very much a part of the show. Busty was short and fat with a nose that tilted skywards and a very sound knowledge of his job. There were no flies on Busty (even in Egypt).

One day he kindly took me down to the Mousky to look for some material I had to get for my Mexican dress. Busty was very proud of his Arabic — '*Shufty* [show] this', '*shufty* that', he would say in a loud and important voice to the shopkeepers. Both in Egypt and in India I much enjoyed the mixture of Arabic or Hindi flavoured with British swear words ENSA bus drivers and stage managers used when addressing the locals — 'You bloody well *shtana schwiar* [wait a bit].'

'Can't you *jildi jow* [go quickly], blast you?' and so on.

* * *

Our opening night was at a Royal Army camp at Abassia.

When I saw the size of the stage my heart sank. We had a tiny dressing room for the seven of us women to get ready in, and next to no space for hanging up all our costumes. There was the usual bucket arrangement behind a wooden screen — the same in all ENSA theatre dressing rooms, and everybody always used to sing to ease the embarrassment of whoever was behind the screen at the time.

We sat on forms, squeezed tightly together to apply our make-up by the dim light.

'Why did you join ENSA Renée?' asked one of the four women in honest wonder. Renée chuckled with enjoyment, but did not say.

The show went down well. It was definitely a popular success, though the camp audiences around Cairo were always hard to please. It was so easy for them to get into town that they had become blasé and it seemed a waste to give them camp shows when they seemed to have comparatively little appreciation of them and they meant so much to men in isolated stations with no other form of entertainment. But the Cairo area was useful for trying out shows to see how various numbers went down and whether people were rightly cast.

Once the performance was over, we would pack up and then be taken to a mess for drinks and sandwiches where we were supposed to make ourselves agreeable.

* * *

These messes after the show were an established custom with overseas ENSA parties, regarded by some as an irksome part of the job and by others as its redeeming feature — 'lots of drinks with nice officers'. I inclined more to the former point of view, though I could enjoy a mess very much if I met someone interesting to talk to or if there were dancing and singing and I was feeling in a party mood. But usually, after having done a show and sat and talked for an hour in the mess, I had no more vitality left; I began to feel very tired and conversation became an effort. However, the teddy bears enjoyed their beer and whisky, the four young women their officers and Renée her story telling, so the company tended to stay until late in the night.

Mess conversations usually went along the following lines. First, 'what will you have to drink?' then, that being settled, 'how long have you been out here?'

'How long do you stay out?'

'What's old England like now?'

'Were you dancing before the war?'

'Where do you go to from here?'

'What sort of journey did you have out from Blighty?'

This last one was a break for me and I played the shipwreck for all it was worth.

* * *

The show played at camps around Cairo for about a month — Almazza, Helwan, Abassia, Heliopolis and Mena. Each evening we would set out to a camp by coach, usually leaving at around six o'clock, and return at about twelve or one o'clock in the morning. I found it difficult to adapt to the small stages and it seemed flat having to dance to two pianos after having been used to an orchestra. Also, one needed to get accustomed to a soldier audience and at first I was not at all happy about my performances, at least not until I realized that it was impossible to give one's best as a ballet dancer under camp theatre conditions and learnt to relax, not to bother too much about technique but to rely on vitality to 'get across'. From a professional point of view, a year with ENSA was a year wasted, but in every other way it was the fullest and richest year one could hope to spend.

In the camp dressing rooms, while we were making up all in a huddle, love affairs were the chief topic of our conversations. Kay, Stephie and Diana (the last had become engaged on the way out) would chatter away to Renée. Pauline, the fourth woman, was usually silent. Renée would read us letters from an Egyptian admirer of hers who covered pages about her 'blue eyes', sending Renée off into fits of mirth, and the singer Gladys would tell us of the presents the manager of the opera house, another Egyptian, kept giving her. We all thought that she was asking for trouble by accepting them, but Gladys took it all very lightly.

'She's dull, she's married,' Renée would say about me.

10

At Your Service:
Rehearsing for Another
Show

L eslie Julian Jones, who made his name writing music
and lyrics for 'intimate' revues at the Ambassadors
Theatre, had come out from England with the rest of
us on the *Marnix*. He was thin, tall, black-haired and
bespectacled, and moved with a limp. He had a charming
personality and undoubtedly a brilliant and inventive mind.
ENSA had asked him to put on a really sophisticated revue
for the Middle East troops, for requests had come in for
more 'West End' types of entertainment. As a consequence,
At Your Service was produced at the Globe Theatre in
Alexandria with Inga Anderson, Victoria Hopper and Chile
Boucher heading the bill.

For some reason, it did not quite catch on, so it was taken
off, rehearsed again and bits taken out here and put in there
before the show reopened at the Cairo Opera House. The
ENSA authorities still did not consider it quite good enough
to perform for the troops, so they withdrew it again to
reproduce before being sent off to India where the troops
were badly in need of entertainment, ENSA having only just
started out there, and required a big production.

By now the stars at the top of the bill had decided that

they had done enough war work and had retired. Renée came in to replace Chile Boucher, and I to replace Beatrice Appleyard, the principal dancer, who was going to form an act with Leslie Julian Jones and Lou Anne Shaw. Renée wanted to go to India, in fact she had originally volunteered with that intention, but I was horrified when I was first told that I was wanted for this show. My husband had just succeeded in getting himself posted to Cairo and companies did not go to India for fewer than six months.

* * *

I went off to see Colonel Newman. I wanted to ask him if I could be put into another show that would remain in the Middle East so that at least occasionally I would be likely to pass through Cairo and at any rate could spend my leaves there.

Colonel Newman was head of the production section. He was a man I grew to like and respect very much. I liked him because of his kindness and consideration and respected him for his cleverness and efficiency.

He had a great knack for managing people. While always kind and always tactful, in the end he invariably got people to do what he wanted.

He pointed out to me that he could promise that I would be in Cairo for at least another six weeks because first the entire show would have to be rerehearsed and then we would have to wait for a ship to become available to take us to India. On the other hand, if I did not go I might be sent off to join another show straight away. Also, this was going to be a good production and they wanted a good ballet dancer for it, so I would be helping ENSA very much.

So I therefore finished up by agreeing to go. It was the same story with the four other women already in the show. None of them wanted to go to India and all of them went off to Newman's office quite firmly resolved to refuse to go (our Middle East contract did not bind us to India). Three out of the four left his office having signed on for six months. 'Shows were needed for the men out there so badly'; 'they would be doing the colonel a great personal service if they went.'

In his case, persuasion was always triumphant over force. A story about Colonel Newman I particularly liked was his reply to a certain young lady who was complaining bitterly about being sent to Iraq in the middle of the summer.

'But don't you realize Colonel, it is 110°F in the shade up there?' 'Don't you worry about that my dear,' he said, 'there isn't any shade there.'

So *At Your Service* was rerehearsed once more. Nearly everything in it was changed apart from the very amusing BBC sketch at the end. But still this was not to be the final *At Your Service*. After we had rehearsed and all the new costumes had been made, the show was tried out at one or two of the Cairo area camps and it was decided that it was still not quite the sort of thing to give the troops, and more numbers would have to be taken out and more 'hammy' ones put in.

Now, usually when you start 'mooking aboot' with a show, as our Blackpool pianist Jack would have put it, you will never make it a success, but curiously enough this final version of *At Your Service* went down extremely well in India. It certainly had something in it for all tastes from the broad, blue gags of the comedian Jack to the subtle and clever characterizations in Renée's bride number (bluish too, but perhaps more an Eton blue), from the sophisticated songs of the very attractive Joan Mathews (the same Joan who had kept the lorries waiting all morning in Phillipville and who had majestically commandeered the area commander's car in Kasr el Nil barracks for us after our wedding) to the baritone Frank's straightforward renderings of 'Rose Marie' and 'The Road to the Island'.

Again, there were all types of dancing in the show from

Connie's tap with the four young women in *Rhythm on Your Toes*, to the little Dégas ballet to Poulenc's music, which Beatrice Appleyard had arranged with me in the part of a dancing mistress taking a class with my pupils.

Of course I was delighted that we were doing this little ballet because I had not expected to get a chance with ENSA of doing anything approaching a real ballet.

* * *

Drury Lane had by now sent me out a dozen pairs of new pointe shoes and my best friend had sent me a parcel that included six bottles of tennis racquet gut reviver, which is invaluable for hardening the blocks of ballet shoes once they get soft.

I opened this parcel, I remember, during a rehearsal and exclaimed with delight, 'Hooray, my gut reviver has arrived,' sending Leslie Julian Jones into fits of mirth.

Leslie, who was patient, kind and very nice to work for, took the morning rehearsals for the sketches, songs, opening and finale. In the afternoon Beatrice took us for the dancing numbers, and Lou Anne Shaw for *Nursery Rhymes*, which I am sorry to say was cut out afterwards (not that I thought it was quite the right thing for soldiers, though the music of jazzed-up nursery rhymes was extremely clever), but I did love my Little Bo Peep ballet frock.

Of course there was the usual 'someone singing and young things flitting' number, with Frank the baritone as the singer, but it was infinitely superior to *Daffodils* with Leslie's *Love in a Mist* music, Beatrice's simple and graceful arrangement and our flowing white chiffon dresses. Mine had long bishop's sleeves and an embroidered waistband in dark blue; the others' frocks were sleeveless with low-cut necklines. Our costumes for the ballet, knee-length white tarlatan dresses with coloured flowers and sashes, mine pink with black velvet bows, a black silk shawl and tiny little hat

71

with a veil were quite charming and we went into ecstasies of joy over them. The dresses helped to reconcile the women to the ballet, which they grumbled about having to do because they felt self-conscious about it.

'Haven't done any ballet for donkey's years,' Brenda would grunt in her curiously deep voice.

'Well neither have I my dear,' Peggy would chime in. Jean, who had trained under Madame Sokolova, was, like me, very pleased at the thought of doing a 'bit of ballet', but as for Joy, Frank's wife, she had never done any ballet at all and so Beatrice had to leave her out of the number. Poor Joy, it was hard on her, she was really a showgirl and not a dancer at all. She could not pick up *Rhythm in Your Toes*, so was left with next to nothing to do in the show. It was all we could do to teach her the comparatively simple movements of *Love in a Mist*. Peggy, Brenda and Jean had not wanted her to join them when the fourth dancer, Jill, had decided not to go to India, for one weak dancer always pulls down the rest, but Frank was needed for the show, Joy was his wife and Frank was not going without her, so that was that.

* * *

What a nervous state we were all in on that first night when we opened, how miserable we were when the show did not seem to be going down well and how completely fed up we were when it was taken off again for more alterations.

Leslie Julian Jones felt more exasperated than anyone, for he then retired from the scene leaving Ivan Campbell to 'do what he liked with the damned show'.

So out came this, that and the other (thank heaven the ballet was spared) and in went some already tried, tested and proven to be popular material, which we thought at first so ordinary and afterwards were forced to accept seemed to be what was wanted. So we all got ready again

for another 'opening' and a second 'shufty' by Colonel
Newman, which actually never came off because our
passages suddenly came through for India and we had to
leave straight away.

11

Passage to India: Sailing from Suez to Bombay

I t was a terrible wrench to leave. My husband and I had
been granted permission by our respective superior
officers to live 'out' and ENSA had allowed me a living
allowance of £6 a week (the cost of my keep at the hotel) in
addition to my salary. All ENSA artistes were given their
keep abroad, but the top salary paid to anyone was £10 a
week. Even stars like Vera Lynn received no more. Renée
never found it enough: she had been used to being paid a
star's salary in London revues, but to me, coming from a
ballet company with somewhat irregular engagements, the
£8 a week I got as a principal dancer on top of my keep
made me feel wonderfully secure and prosperous.

* * *

We were also allowed to use the NAAFI. Over this, some
members of a band who came out to the Middle East for
three weeks caused a lot of ill feeling by so taking advantage
of the non-couponed clothing at reasonable prices that they
bought up NAAFI's entire stock.

The NAAFI was the real envy of the Egyptians. When
Egypt eventually decided to enter the war on the side of the
Allies six months before the last trump sounded, the
Egyptian officers rubbed their hands together and said:

'Ah now we can use the NAAFI.'

* * *

On the morning of 18 March 1944 our company of 12 left Cairo by train for Port Tewfic. We left early and, as it was only a short journey through desert country, we arrived at Tewfic with most of the day to spare. We heard that we would be going on board that evening at about five o'clock, which was when our ship was expected to come down the canal. It would sail alone to Aden where it would join a convoy for the crossing of the Indian Ocean.

We hung around the French club until lunch time, then continued to hang around until tea time before at last it was time to walk down the long straight road bordering the canal to change our money (piastres to rupees), check our luggage and be ready to embark as soon as the ship arrived. I was feeling acutely miserable, the day had seemed interminably long and I was thankful for something to do at last. Our ship was very late getting in, so we sat outside the post official's little cabin and waited while the sun gradually went down, the sky darkened and the air grew chilly.

Renée, who had been feeling ill and gloomy all through the day, suddenly burst into the gayest of moods, and started telling stories and rhymes to an audience consisting of all of us, two officer friends of Peggy's and Brenda's who had come to see them off and anyone else who happened to be around.

It was very nearly dark before our ship arrived down the Suez Canal. Many other ships had been passing all the time, and, as each drew alongside, we wondered: 'Is this the one?'

We liked the look of the *City of Exeter*. It was small and painted white. There was nothing warlike about it and, to my relief, it did not in the least resemble the *Marnix*.

We all got into a little tugboat and chugged off to the ship's side through the choppy waves. It was quite dark as we climbed the gangway to come aboard and a wind was sweeping over the water.

* * *

Jean and I found that we were to be in a cabin together, just us two. It was tiny, but would have been nice had it been better ventilated. However, the *City of Exeter* was by no means a new ship and it was very poorly ventilated. With its porthole windows screwed down, I dreaded what it would be like in the cabin later on when we reached the Red Sea.

There was a pleasant drawing room and a dining saloon, a quarter the size of the one on the *Marnix* but one I liked much better because it was not down below and we could watch the sea through the portholes at meal times.

It was such a wonderful sea, too, so calm and blue, and there were flying fish to watch, leaping unconcernedly in and out of the water and sometimes a school of porpoises would pass by, plunging, black shining bodies appearing and disappearing at the ship's side.

The *City of Exeter* was not a troop carrier. It had a cargo of Spitfire parts down below and there were only about two hundred passengers on board, 70 United States Air Force officers who had embarked with us, a group of Admiralty personnel bound for Ceylon, some Quaker Red Cross workers, and a good many civilians — wives going out to join their husbands in India — and others.

* * *

The most interesting person I met was Rik (Sir Mortimer Wheeler), an archaeologist brigadier who was travelling to India to take up a responsible position in the field of Indian archaeology. We later made friends and my conversations with him are my most pleasant memories of that voyage. He had a fund of experiences about which to talk and a great sense of humour. He was intensely energetic, both mentally and physically, and possessed a masterful self-assurance without the slightest trace of pose or conceit. He combined the sensitivity and sensibility of an artist with the unexpected hardness, to me at any rate, of a military outlook. He was, to a remarkable degree, that rare combination of a man of action and a man of intellect combined in one person.

A young Scotswoman travelling with her three-year old daughter to join her missionary husband at Port Sudan occupied the cabin opposite ours. The child had never seen her father and was wildly excited. She was a very sweet little girl without a vestige of shyness. It was surprising she did not get spoilt on board, given the amount of attention everyone gave her, but her mother managed to steer her clear of that. During morning boat drill, which was a very easygoing affair on board the *City of Exeter* — there was no lining up on the deck and standing there for half an hour but merely going to the lounge and sitting in armchairs until the second bell rang — in a life jacket that quite swamped her little Carol would toddle about explaining to us all what it was all about.

'If the ship breaks down, you see, we all get into the boats and row to another ship, and we wear these jackets to keep our backs warm.'

* * *

The 70 United States Air Force officers on board were a very pleasant bunch. Speaking for myself, Joan and Hank, the pianist, whom the Americans had rescued after the shipwreck and then later flown to Cairo on a *baksheesh* trip, we felt very well disposed towards all of them, but I think Renée voiced the opinion of a good many of the others when she said that, from what she had seen of Americans in London, she would not have believed how agreeable they could be.

You certainly cannot judge a people from the way their

soldiers behave in foreign cities in wartime. In uniform for the first time and with money in their pockets, newly enlisted soldiers will often fling their weight about wherever and whoever they are. Everyone knows, too, how a steady English businessman will let himself go while on holiday in Paris when he is out of his accustomed shell and in a foreign city where nobody knows his day-to-day character.

I got to know one young American called Jack quite well on board. He was what a Hollywood producer might call 'a fine specimen of clean-limbed, healthy, upright, American manhood'. Always pleasant, smiling and well mannered, he would talk on and on about his country.

'Well, has he sold you America yet?' my brigadier archaeologist friend Rik would ask me.

* * *

Then there were the civilians. I remember a conversation I had on the voyage with a woman whose husband was in India. The war had prevented her from returning earlier and she was sick and tired of England and longing to be back in India.

'They made me do war work,' she said, raising delicate eyebrows in horror at the thought, 'I, who have never done a stroke of work in my life.'

'Well, it was about time you started, then,' I felt like saying, and went off thinking that this would probably be the general attitude to expect from *memsahib*s in India. Later, when I had been in India for a while, I became more tolerant, for I began to realize that with so many servants foisted on one because of the caste system — the butler will not cook, the cook will not sweep out a room and so on — white women in India are almost forced into an idle life, becoming part of the caste system themselves, and more and more start to take their idleness for granted.

I heard a great deal of criticism from soldiers in India of

English wives who were doing so little for their countrymen and the war effort on the whole, though there were undoubtedly individuals who did their utmost, but I am sure that the majority's attitude of taking their inactivity entirely for granted was largely responsible.

* * *

There was no hanging about in port on this voyage. The next morning, when the little, dark, bustling steward came into our cabin to unscrew the windows, we looked out over a stretch of azure-blue sea to the sandy hills on the Egyptian coastline lying white in the strong sunlight.

We were sailing down the Gulf of Suez with the land clearly visible on either side of the ship. The air was fresh and warm, and everything seemed so pretty and bright on board with all the white paint and light cretonne covers and curtains in the saloons. There was a pleasant feeling of intimacy among the passengers: since there were comparatively few of them everyone got to know everyone else, at any rate by sight.

We sailed out of the Gulf of Suez and into the Red Sea, and every day became hotter. Our little cabin was stifling and I began to think about sleeping out on deck. Rik had a lilo bed, which he kindly let me borrow; so I would take my pitch at nightfall, make my bed, later undress in the cabin, put on a coat over my nightie and slip out onto the deck, complete with life belt and 'panic bag'.

As time went on, more and more people took to sleeping out, some only on a rug on the deck boards. After a while it became quite difficult to find a good pitch for oneself. The nights were very dark, so I had no idea who my neighbour was going to be when, half asleep, I heard scuffling and breathing and a bed being arranged a few yards off.

It was amusing to wake up in the morning and see who else was there.

I remember once waking up with a pair of boots nearly in my face. They belonged to handsome Captain Flemming, the second in command of the US airmen on board.

The majority of the Americans, however, preferred their cabins, hot as they were. After the camp near Naples, which was from where they had all come, it was such a relief, they explained, to sleep in nice comfortable bunks with soft sheets and mattresses, and they were not going to turn out on a hard deck for anyone.

How beautiful those nights were, though, with no moon but thousands upon thousands of stars. The sky seems so much further off in the East than it appears to be in England and so wonderfully clear.

The dark water, the waves tipped with phosphorescence, swept softly by at the ship's side, its lapping and swishing lulling me to sleep each night.

The morning would come with a start. 'Scuse please,' the native deck scrubbers would cry, sloshing buckets of water about, and you had to get up quickly if you did not want a drenching.

How good breakfast tasted after a night in the open and a cool seawater bath as we sat down to delicious crisp little rolls, eggs and coffee.

* * *

Our company had rehearsals every morning in a low-roofed cabin somewhere down in the stern, at least until the Urdu class, which always arrived too early and hovered before we had properly finished, would push us out. We were expected to give a show sometime during the voyage and, with the weather becoming hotter and hotter each day, it was not something to which any of us were looking forward.

Joan was already feeling quite knocked out and ill from the heat, and lay on her bunk most of the day, and Renée was coming out all over in that horrible irritating rash known as prickly heat, from which nearly all of us were to suffer later on.

* * *

We passed the islands of the Twelve Apostles, white hills of sand and rock rising from the water, remote, lifeless, but strangely compelling. We stopped at Port Sudan, where I was struck by the contrast between the extreme fatness of the white-suited and topped Europeans and the extreme thinness of the bushy-haired, coal-black African natives on the dockside. Here little Carol, in tussore dress and tiny topi, met her daddy with the entire ship's company leaning over the rails to watch the great meeting and, since he was so obviously not the daddy of her imagination at all, she clung to her mother in an agony of shyness and suspicion.

Aden lay under its bare sun-baked rock. The desert across the harbour shimmered in a haze of heat and the native bumboats came bobbing out to us over the water with their coloured baskets and slippers, and fresh fruit for sale. We did not go into port, much to Jack's disappointment, for he was dying to go to the American club there to get his teeth into a real hamburger.

We soon left Aden behind and started off across the Indian Ocean.

* * *

Amusements were almost immediately in full swing on board. There were dances on deck in the late afternoon, but these did not really catch on, for the radio loudspeakers were weak and at any rate it soon got too hot to want to dance. There was housey-housey (bingo), a brains' trust and a rival quiz between the sexes, which was very amusing and in which, I believe, the women came out on top. Then of course there was our show, but I have not quite reached that horror yet. In the Red Sea we had played deck tennis at sunset, when the sea all round became suffused with the soft red light that seemed to justify its name.

* * *

Now, the biggest diversion for keeping the passengers occupied during the day was the 'submarine watch'. The captain had asked for volunteers to watch from the four corners of the boat deck. Rik said that the procedure was:

First, a torpedo hit the ship.

Second, you saw the submarine.

Third, you gave the alarm as the ship went down.

The captain had decided not to wait for the convoy at Aden and we had set off across the Indian Ocean unescorted save for a solitary aeroplane that came and looked us up (or rather down) once daily and then buzzed off again. The *City of Exeter*'s maximum speed was 13 knots, and there were no submarine detectors on board.

After my recent experience I must say that I felt unhappy about this and it was partly because I was nervous that I preferred to sleep on deck where I had more chance of jumping overboard if the ship were torpedoed — but then there was the thought of sharks. We had seen them in Aden harbour and thrown bits of bread down to them, hoping to see them turn over to swallow them. However, they did not seem to fancy anything we threw them; someone suggested we should lower a menu to them — a chopped-off hand or foot would probably have been most to their taste.

* * *

The *City of Exeter* was in the middle of the Indian Ocean, and only a day or two's journey from Bombay before we gave the first performance of the fourth and final edition of *At Your Service*.

In the morning they heaved all the dress boxes up from out of the hold and onto the deck and we unpacked them there in the burning sun. We then carried armfuls of costumes down to the cabins to spend an even hotter time ironing them out ready for the show.

Renée told us, with deep disgust, how on her third journey down from the deck with her arms piled with dresses and her face streaming from the heat, she had passed a lady passenger reclining in a deck chair in the shade, a glass of cordial on a table at her side, who had smiled sweetly and asked:

'Getting excited about tonight?'

* * *

The show took place in the dining saloon after the second sitting for dinner was over. It was a low and not very large saloon and of course the portholes had been screwed down since sunset.

The stage had been rigged up at the farther end from the two doors and we dressed behind curtains. The audience completely packed the place and no fresh air at all reached the stage — the fans overhead were just churning out hot stale gases.

On top of all this I could not help thinking that, if a torpedo should hit the ship, not many people would stand a chance of getting out through those two doors, least of all the performers.

After the opening number, perspiration was pouring down our faces and our make-up was running off in streams, our hair hanging down, wringing wet. I went on for my Mexican dance with the brim of my large straw hat flapping down like two spaniel's ears — I had to lift it up to see the audience — my face the colour of a beetroot.

Poor Renée did not know how to get into her bride's dress with its long tight-fitting sleeves and Joan's beautifully arranged piled-up coiffure looked as if she had just come out of a steamy bathroom.

However, despite all this the audience enjoyed the show, which they proved by going out and changing their wringing shirts in the interval and then returning in full force to see the second half of the programme.

The ballet, which came in this half, was almost impossible to perform on the tiny rocking stage, with all of us gasping for air like goldfish out of water. All in all, I do not think I have ever given such a shocking performance in my life, or been more thankful when one was over.

There was a last-minute panic followed by a hasty whisper to Jack to play the Star Spangled Banner after God Save the King because half our audience was American.

Hardly any of us other than Jean knew the words, and she even got them wrong. With a straight face, I opened and shut my mouth and lustily sang nothing.

12

Bombay and Meeting the Renowned Ram Gopal

I remember the morning when we first sighted land and then slowly sailed into Bombay harbour. The water, which became a muddy greenish yellow colour, was sprinkled with islands and native craft. In the distance were the hills of the mainland and over on our left the houses and domes of Bombay island itself gradually rose into view.

I stood watching from the deck rail with Rik and Jack who were continuing an argument they had begun the previous day over whether the products of human genius were of relatively greater value than the lives of ordinary soldiers. In addition to the active part he had been playing in Italy as a brigade commander, Rik had been working for the preservation of works of art from war damage, whereas Jack held that he had joined the war to fight for what he understood was democracy.

Rik held that if it were a question of sacrificing human lives to save the paintings of, for example, Giotto, it should be done because human lives are replaceable — not speaking individually of course — whereas Giotto's paintings are not.

Jack, who was a young upholder of democracy and of the rights of man, was deeply shocked at this point of view and could not understand how anyone could consider that a picture 'however beautiful, you know,' could even for a moment be considered to hold more value than a human life.

While Bombay city drew closer and closer Rik was becoming more and more irritated with Jack and Jack increasingly shocked by Rik.

* * *

The great archway of the Gateway of India dominated the waterfront with, further along, the high dome of the Taj Mahal Hotel. We sailed past the Gateway and then through a lock into port. Great ships lay all around and tugs, with names such as *Willing* and *Able* painted on their sterns, chugged busily about.

The heat seemed to rise up in a suffocating blanket as we left the sea breeze behind. The dockside was swarming with coolies. They seemed such tiny men after the strapping Egyptian *fellahin*, so monkey-like and wiry. I watched a native overseer superintending one lot of coolies with a whip in one hand and a fiendish gleam in his aged eye.

The women coolies were a depressing sight. There was a grim, sexless, ageless look about their hard wrinkled faces and scraggy overworked bodies. They were dressed in a hideous garment that wound round the hips and then was passed through the legs to tuck in at the waist, but it was the expression of loathing and bitterness on their faces that struck me most forcibly as they trudged to and fro carrying heavy sacks on their heads, the dust from the sacks hanging on the air and making their skins white in patches.

* * *

Everybody on board had lunched early, before we came into port, and now it was time for us to say our goodbyes. In turn, everyone left the ship — the civilians, the Americans, the Admiralty workers and the Quakers. But nobody, however, came to fetch the ENSA party. We waited on and on, sitting on the deck in the burning heat and not in the best of tempers. Eventually, the ENSA officer, a young bespectacled lieutenant, turned up and explained that, unaware of the *City of Exeter*'s early arrival, they had not been expecting us for two or three days.

* * *

We then piled into a couple of waiting ENSA vans and watched our luggage being loaded onto a lorry before being driven off for our first glimpses of the streets of Bombay.

Although it was only the end of March, the heat seemed intense and I felt appalled at the thought of what it might be like later on. At that point I did not know that April and May are the two hottest months in Bombay, with the monsoon breaking in June and lasting until September.

The trees in the streets along which we drove were in full leaf, brilliantly green, with vivid splashes of colour from the blossoms in people's gardens and up the walls of their houses. Being open to view as they were, with windows set well back behind wide wooden verandas, they reminded me of dolls' houses. Because the roofed verandas prevent the sun's rays from shining directly into the rooms, hardly any bungalows or houses in India are built without them.

Later we turned into a wide main street in which the essentially Victorian British architecture was adorned with Indian ornamentation. The pavements were thickly populated with slim, small, shiny black-haired and white-suited Indians of superior castes, Hindus of a lower order in loose cotton shirts and round caps, half naked beggars sitting on the pavement or whining in the gutter, and small beautiful women with coloured saris and coils of black hair, a flower tucked into the bun at the back. Then, of course, there was a fair sprinkling of British civilians and, in even larger numbers, members of HM and US forces.

87

It was refreshing to keep glimpsing the sea at the ends of the streets — Bombay is built on what is virtually a long narrow island. This certainly adds to the coolness and attraction of the town, though I wished they had pulled down the British architecture of the previous century. I did not want to be reminded of Birmingham in Bombay.

* * *

Though the drive to the hostel where we were to be put up took only about ten minutes, Peggy and Brenda had already decided that they did not like Bombay and wished that they had never come.

Poor Peggy and Brenda were to feel this even more strongly by the next morning. The hostel, though a palace compared with the one at Phillipville, was rather dingy and we found that we would be horribly crowded there. The bespectacled lieutenant attributed our conditions to the unexpectedness of our arrival and said that if the *City of Exeter* had waited for the convoy at Aden we would have got in much later at a time when Bombay would have been less crowded. But he reassured us that the arrangement was only temporary and that we would all be moved to hotels during the next few days.

And, indeed, Jean and I were soon moved to a private flat owned by some people called Trollop, who were friends of the billeting officer.

* * *

On that first evening in Bombay I walked by myself down to the seafront by the Gateway of India. The view over the harbour was very beautiful with the little boats, the islands and the calm sea lying in the soft evening light.

Jean and I unpacked and went to bed early, but Peggy and Brenda went out with three Americans off the ship who were stationed for the time being at a camp a little way out of the city.

After they had all spent a good evening together, the men could not find a taxi willing to take them all the way back to the camp, so the women suggested that, since the men were unfamiliar with the town, they return with them to the hostel to sleep on beds in Ivan's and Jack's room.

* * *

I have not yet mentioned Ivan. He was a man of middle age, short and rather stout with greying hair and very kindly grey eyes. He was an old friend of Jean's family and they always joined the same companies so that he could look after her, though really she could wind him round her little finger. Although he had worked in repertory, Ivan was not a professional. He possessed a private income upon which he could retire at any time he chose to become a gentleman of leisure. He had the sweetest and mildest of tempers, so Rik had christened him 'Ivan the Terrible'. Unfortunately, though, he had no sense of tact whatsoever. He explained to the good lady who ran the hostel that the three gentlemen of the US Air Force, who had appeared that morning at the breakfast table, were 'friends the girls had met the evening before and invited back for the night'.

The landlady, not unnaturally, had formed her own conclusions from this explanation and had rung up Colonel Dunstan at the ENSA office to lodge a horrified report. Peggy and Brenda had been sent for immediately.

When I returned for lunch I found the two of them and Jean sitting round the table and lamming into poor Ivan, who sat there, mournful and penitent, looking like a beaten spaniel.

* * *

I had spent an exciting morning going to the Taj Mahal Hotel to meet Rik who had spent the night as a guest at Government House and who had turned up with one of the governor's ADCs whom, to my great surprise, was an old Oxford friend of my brother's.

Michael had been a captain in the guards, but in a horrible accident in which a mine had exploded in his face he had lost the sight of one eye and was no longer fit for active service. He wore a patch over the eye and a little pointed fair beard, for the explosion had also injured his chin. With his pale sensitive face, these disguises only added to the interest and individuality of his looks, though he obviously felt self conscious about them.

After a drink at the Taj Mahal Hotel, he took us both round with him to visit Ram Gopal, a dancer with whom he was on quite friendly terms.

* * *

I had admired Ram Gopal's dancing immensely when I had seen him with his troupe in London, and so was delighted at the thought of meeting him in person, and on my first day in India too.

We went to his studio where – in a brown and gold dressing gown – he received us very simply and unpretentiously. He spoke English extremely well and his conversation was quiet and intelligent. After a time, we went to a woman dancer's studio and watched her rehearsing with some of her pupils.

She was a beautiful dancer, combining dignity and poise with a sensuous litheness and possessing wonderful bodily control from her ever-moving black eyes and eyebrows to her fingers, soft and powerful, curling back from her palms.

That was, unfortunately, the last I was to see of Rik, for he went on to Delhi the next day, though I met Michael again several times.

* * *

A few days later Michael asked me out to the ADC bungalow at Government House, which was situated right on the tip of land that juts out into the sea at the end of Malabar Bay, a beautiful spot. The ADCs were very fortunate — they each had a couple of cool peaceful rooms in the bungalow from where they could look right out over the sea, with nothing between them and it but a brilliant border of scarlet flowers.

Michael apologized for an unexpected visitor, an Indianized Polish woman wearing a sari who was going to instruct him in yoga, and he remained talking to her while I borrowed a bathing dress of his, which I managed to pin in such a way that it covered me adequately, and went down a heavily shaded path with thick vegetation on either side to the governor's private beach for a swim. Michael sent a grave and turbaned manservant to accompany me.

It was wonderful floating in that warm blue water looking out at the city across the bay. I thought of my last bathe, in a cove near Torquay with foaming waves beating against the rocks. It had been only at the end of the previous September yet seemed decades ago now.

* * *

There would be no shows in the first week, for it had become apparent from the performance on board ship that some of the costumes we had brought with us were too warm for an Indian summer. An officer on the ENSA staff in Bombay, Jack Hawkins, came to help us rehearse. He was charming and we all liked him enormously.

The men had to have light blue linen dinner jackets made to replace their cloth ones and they looked very nice with their black trousers; and we women had to have thin dresses made for the opening.

* * *

Meanwhile, Jean and I were getting along quite nicely with our host and hostess and their daughter, who was in the Wrens. Mr Trollop was very comfortably off, having made his money out of electric trams. His wife was an extremely energetic little woman who had organized and built up a soldiers' canteen at the town hall, with meals and snacks off a counter, easy chairs and papers, ping-pong tables, dart boards and even a first aid section. All this, she had done on her own initiative and the troops greatly appreciated it, for they were pitifully neglected in India. They were without NAAFIs, without ENSA until a few months before, and with next to nothing done officially for their comfort and recreation.

Mrs Trollop had certainly done magnificently. Jean and I would sometimes go along to the canteen in the morning to help her; it was a far cry from the canteen work I had known in England because there were native servants to do all the washing up and dirty work, but then, with the temperature getting on for 100°F, even cutting sandwiches is an effort.

* * *

We had daily rehearsals. We also had to go for fittings for the new costume and to be measured for our tropical kit. The latter consisted of bush jackets, slacks and skirts, but we were also provided with topis, heavy shoes and mackintoshes for the monsoons, and sleeping bags, complete with bedding, mosquito nets and bags of Bakelite eating utensils. These utensils all broke on the first journey and Joan raised a howl of laughter when she first undid her bag before an admiring ring of officers, announcing proudly, 'this is my equipment,' as she shook out a bagful of broken pieces.

We also had to go three times for cholera inoculations, but

all the same we managed to fit in a very good time between these various activities.

* * *

Our American friends swarmed into town and took us off to indulge in enormous luscious ice creams at the Taj Mahal Hotel. They had all been provided with little books of notes on the correct prices to pay in town and the right amount to tip. This arose from the infinitely less well-paid British soldiers having complained that the Americans were raising prices wherever they went through their lavish and unquestioning spending. It was amusing to see them responding to a tonga-driver demanding five rupees for his fare. After fumbling in their pockets, they would produce the booklet, look up the right page and then say, 'Oh no, this says ...'

There were plenty of lovely swimming clubs in Bombay, including the Cricket Club, the Willingdon and the Beach Candy, but I must say that the bathes I enjoyed most were the ones in the sea off the governor's beach, and out at Jehu, where the Trollops sometimes took Jean and me on a Sunday. There, a long narrow strip of country green with palms ran out into the sea, and the waves broke on wide sandy beaches.

The Trollops owned one of the many straw-covered huts (or bashers as they were called) that lay dotted about under the palm trees. We spent the whole day there, on the beach, in the little flower-filled garden, or under the shade of the straw-covered veranda.

Jean and I both found ourselves in difficulties at the clubs over the rule that it was compulsory to wear bathing caps, for we did not possess a single one between us and they were unprocurable in the Bombay shops.

At the Cricket Club, where Jean liked to swim every afternoon with Ivan, the bath officials, with a typically eastern interpretation of European rules, which insisted on following the letter of the law, would not even permit ladies in the bath with their hair tied up in a scarf.

I suggested that Jean put the top of an old silk stocking of mine on her head, bringing the leg part round under her chin and tucking in the foot.

She told me afterwards, with delight, how as she had swum along in the water the superintendent had followed her along the entire edge of the pool constantly questioning her about the cap and how she had replied:

'It's the very latest kind from America.'

It made us indignant, though, to see the Sikhs bathing. Certainly, they tucked their topknots into caps, but their black beards were allowed to trail unrestrictedly in the water.

* * *

Because we were staying in so many different places we saw very little of the other members of the company other than at rehearsals, but I believe everyone was having a good time and accepting invitations to bathing parties, to parties at the yacht club, or to dinners and dances in the air-conditioned ballrooms of the Taj Mahal Hotel.

My husband had generously said that I might go out as much as I liked, so I did and I enjoyed myself.

I remember being taken to a lovely fair one evening in aid of the beggars of Bombay. It was held in one of the many parks under trees covered in a dazzling mass of shining coloured lights. Beneath were stalls, sideshows, a band for dancing and a cabaret. There was a jungle of bamboo filled with live animals and birds and a long ladder leading up one tree to where a fortune-teller sat in a little hut in the branches.

13

Mard Island: Performances and Mess Parties

I did not feel that our first performance, given at an RAF depot in the town, was much of an improvement on the one we had given on board ship. Although we did at least have ventilation, my face poured with sweat as soon as I started to dance, I felt quite exhausted after two minutes and was unable to give a good performance, which, as always, threw me into a deep depression. I did not realize how, after a time, one gets used to dancing in the heat and even begins to think nothing of it. In fact, I found it infinitely preferable to dancing in the intense cold, which can be agony on numb toes and with frozen muscles. Iceland would have been the last place I would have volunteered to go with ENSA.

Poor Joan was feeling completely exhausted by the change of climate. She got through the first performance, but her temperature was still very high and she was continually being sick. The doctor made her stay in bed.

Because I had got to know the opening number called *Three Leading Ladies* in which Renée, Connie and Joan, in a dialogue followed by a song, tried to score points off each other as they fanned their professional jealousy, I was asked to take over Joan's part. During rehearsals I had also picked up another number entitled *Handing Over* in which a bus conductor, a postman and a window cleaner were handing their jobs over to women before answering their country's call.

Fortunately, in these numbers one was called upon to speak rather than sing the lines to the music, for otherwise I would never have been able to attempt them. Joan's solo songs were of course cut out for my performances.

I must say I enjoyed speaking on the stage for the first time and felt honoured when Captain Jack Hawkins congratulated me after the show and told me that I had 'got away with it'.

* * *

For the first two weeks we worked at naval, army and air force camps to very appreciative audiences, but it took time before the show became as slick as a revue ought to be. Nonetheless, we were always complimented on our performance after the show. Of course, there were 'after the show' parties in the messes, which were far more spontaneous than the formal parties to which we had been invited in and around Cairo, where the officers were used to and probably bored with entertaining ENSA artists each week.

We gave two open-air performances on the portable stage we were afterwards to take on tour with us.

I hated it for being small and rickety, but it was certainly cool and pleasant to dance in the open-air under the stars.

After the first of the open-air performances, with a tremendously enthusiastic audience that included some Indian troops, we were invited to dine in the mess. The dinner was held in a long wooden building in which rats scampered about the rafters overhead and Jean and I felt quite sick at the thought of them dropping down on to the table. In fact, we could hardly eat the excellent dinner provided.

The rats in Bombay were indomitable. Even in Mrs Trollop's beautiful modern flat I found one of my precious new pairs of ballet shoes gnawed through, and one night Jean saw one of the creatures scamper across the floor of the Taj Mahal Hotel itself while she was dining there with Ivan.

At our second open-air performance, which took place in a dark garden, full of sweet-scented bushes of flowering jasmine, the lights on our portable stage failed — probably through the vibration caused by dancing, and we finished the performance illuminated by the headlamps of cars and lorries driven up all round at the back of the audience.

At another camp there was an outdoor mess after the show at which chairs and little tables of refreshments had been laid out under palm trees hung with tiny coloured lights. There was also a pet monkey, known as Denis, who scampered about grabbing food, pulling everyone's hair, rifling through our handbags and generally entertaining the company.

* * *

Driving home from the camps at night through the streets of Bombay, I was horrified by how many homeless people stretched out to sleep on the pavements.

'Why is it so terrible?' an officer once said to me. 'Surely it is better that they should sleep out in the fresh air than crowded together in back rooms.'

* * *

Fortunately, Joan was well enough to come with us to Mard Island, where we went for three days from Bombay — three of the pleasantest days of the tour. The island had been turned into a training camp, and there were enough men there to justify our staying to give three performances. While Mard was really only an island during the rains, at other times one could reach it by a road that had been built across the marshes, but the quicker way was by ferry.

We went in three carloads, and for the first time we were driven by Indians. I must admit that I was terrified at the reckless speed at which they went. It was no good telling our driver to go slower because he just replied that he must not lose sight of the car in front, which was hurtling along, swerving madly past bullock carts, charging through herds of goats and speeding past every vehicle on the road. Renée and Joan inside did not care a rap; it was Peggy, Joy and I who were to suffer most from the Indian drivers. This was less because of the speed at which they went than because of the feeling they gave us of having no control over their vehicles. We were on edge throughout the journey.

However, we all landed up safely after having bumped along the deeply rutted roads from which the dust rose in clouds. The island was hilly and partially wooded. There were beautiful stretches of sandy beaches with the wonderful wide-open sea scintillating in the sunset beyond.

We were taken to our sleeping quarters, which were separate from the rest of the camp and consisted of a row of little wooden huts facing the sea and the glorious setting sun. We each had a hut to ourselves containing one or two pieces of wooden furniture and a camp bed draped with a mosquito net. There was a little bathroom at the back of each hut and an Indian servant would bring us cans of hot water with which to wash.

Next morning, of course, we all collected at the camp theatre for rehearsals. I was delighted by the stage, which really was a decent size and, in the fresher air out here at Mard, looked forward to the evening's performance with pleasure. Jean and I then went down to the beach, paddled, bathed, danced and turned cartwheels on the sand. We felt like children on a summer holiday.

That feeling stayed with me all the time I was at Mard, and I did not feel inclined to join in the goings-on with the others, the drinking parties, moonlight bathes and rides in the 'duck' in which the others were revelling.

The show was a tremendous success and I think we all enjoyed those three performances enormously. Although the little ballet was not, of course, to everybody's taste by any means, I was very pleased all through our ENSA tour by how much certain individuals seemed to appreciate it. One such person was an Indian naval officer stationed at Mard called Dadaboi.

* * *

Dadaboi possessed an amazing tenor voice. He sang one night at the mess and it was astonishing to hear an Indian sing Italian opera in a voice that soared to the rafters, completely effortless and breathtakingly beautiful, when the only Indian singing I had heard before or since is the continuous whining sound made through the nose that so many Europeans find unattractive.

Dadaboi was, however, an intensely English public school type. While he had the most Oxford accent I have ever heard and beautifully polished manners, he had the looks of an Italian tenor. It seemed astonishing to me that such a Europeanized individual should, as a Parsee Indian, one day after his death be laid out in an enormous circular building open to the sky in the centre of Bombay for the vultures to feed on his flesh.

There was a model of this building in the museum and you could see where the corpses were laid out and where their blood ran down in grooves as the vultures feasted. It was a macabre sight to see them hovering over the building day in day out 'waiting for the flesh that dies'.

Dadaboi told me bitterly how humiliated he had been made to feel when a party of his English friends wanted him to accompany them to a 'European only' place such as Beach Candy swimming pool or the Yachting Club and he, as a high-caste Indian, would be turned away at the door in his own city. I could feel how conscious he was of his high birth from the way he spoke to waiters when he took me out to dinner one night — much as an emperor might speak to his subjects. Later, when he drove me home he sang Santa Lucia at the top of his wonderful voice with the car rocking wildly through the streets of Bombay.

* * *

But this was after we had returned from Mard. Our last night there was the night of a terrible conflagration in Bombay harbour. An ammunition ship exploded and appalling damage was done to warehouses and other buildings with a heavy loss of life. Mr Trollop worked all night at the canteen sending out vans of refreshment to the men fighting the fire on the dockside.

From Mard Island we saw a great red glow in the sky over Bombay and wondered what had happened.

14

Northwest Frontier: Travel to Rawalpindi and Peshawar

Very soon after our return from Mard we set off on a long journey northwards to the Punjab: a whole host of officers, chiefly from Mard Island, thronged the platform to see us off.

We were all wearing our new tropical kit, khaki Aertex blouses and slacks with khaki bandeaux for our hair, which we always kept covered as a protection from dirt when we were travelling.

Indian railway coaches are built on entirely different lines from those in the United Kingdom. I found that I had been allotted quite a spacious sleeping compartment to share with Renée and Joan in which the bunks were placed parallel with the railway lines and with a separate toilet room at one end of the compartment. There was no corridor, so to get to the restaurant car for meals we had to disembark at a station and walk up the platform. This made for a change and gave us a chance to stretch our legs, so we really did not mind at all. The meals were of a higher quality, we thought, than those in England and we enjoyed meeting the rest of the company at mealtimes.

Two Indian bearers had been engaged to travel with us

and they made up our beds. We all travelled with sleeping bags containing our own sheets, blankets and pillow, and these the bearers unrolled and laid out on our bunks. They also brought us our breakfast trays in the morning, but their chief duty was to look after the theatre costumes, which had to be ironed and hung up before each performance. The irons were heavy charcoal-burning ones and it must have been a very hot and tiring job. Thank goodness I never saw them doing what I had seen so many Egyptian ironers do, which was first to fill their mouths with water and then spit it out over the garment to be pressed.

I always enjoyed travelling: I loved the sense of movement and especially of going somewhere I had never been before. The journey was very hot and, in an attempt to keep cool, we used to keep the blinds down in the carriage in the middle of the day. When we stepped out onto the platform to walk up to the restaurant car for lunch, the sun seemed to scorch us through to our skins. We spent most of the rest of our time lying on our bunks reading or dozing. Joan had picked up an outrageous little book from a station bookstall entitled *The Art of Love in the Orient*, which, amid much mirth, she read aloud to us in patches.

* * *

After a two-day journey we arrived at last in Rawalpindi were Captain Bull, tall and lean and cheerful, met us. He was the ENSA officer in charge of the district and was to look after the company all the time we were to be in the Northwest. We were taken off to our respective hotels and again I was put with Jean; we were given a pleasant room in a nice hotel that was built, like nearly all the houses in Rawalpindi, entirely on one floor. We were astonished, though, to find the same primitive toilet arrangements here as at the camp on Mard Island, as indeed we were to find all over India apart from Bombay and Calcutta. I believe

Flashman's Hotel in Rawalpindi was the only one in the Northwest to have bathrooms with water laid on. I was told that one of the reasons why water pipes had not been laid down was that the fetching and carrying of water provided a considerable amount of employment for the lowest class of Indians — the untouchables.

* * *

Poor Jean had to see a doctor in Rawalpindi and, to her great distress, was admitted to hospital and told that she would have to be out of the show for quite a long time. She had strained her back while diving and the physician decided to put her in a plaster jacket and send her up to the hills, to Murray, to recuperate. We ourselves were also due to go to Murray later on, so we told her that we would all be seeing her again fairly soon and that by the time we got there she would be well and fit enough to rejoin the show. Poor Jean, her recovery was to take much longer, though, than even the physician had anticipated.

* * *

Rawalpindi had the same characteristics as all the other places we were to visit in the north: namely there was a native quarter (where we were warned not to go on our own) and a European part. In the latter, long straight roads — the main one was always called 'The Mall' — were lined with prosperous-looking verandaed bungalows standing well back in their own gardens with the club always at the heart of this distinctly suburban community. All these clubs seemed to me to be very much the same — Anglo-Indian society spoke about its 'club life' and its members' lives did in fact gravitate round these clubs. People went there to swim, dance and eat, but principally to gossip and drink. They drank because it was the smart thing to do, because drink was supposed to keep away malaria and because it was a cure for boredom. In the messes, of course, everybody drank as heavily as they did in the clubs and chiefly whisky. Peggy and I, who hated the stuff, developed a way of making one glass spin out for a whole evening. The only woman I remember meeting in India with a really lovely skin told me that she never touched a drop of alcohol but always drank at least ten glasses of water a day.

'I do as the natives do,' she said.

* * *

Our opening performance was, without exaggeration, an enormous success and this success lasted throughout the tour. At the first performance, however, Renée came backstage after her initial appearance snorting and complaining that she had noticed that officers' wives filled all the seats in the entire front row of the audience.

'I didn't come out to India to play to a lot of women,' she announced in disgust. But the crowning insult was that one of them had actually dared to bring her knitting, and she was sitting right in the middle of the front row too, which just about rendered Renée speechless. Afterwards, however, the lady in question apologized profusely for her breach of etiquette. She told us that she had expected to be bored by a second-rate concert party, instead of which she was greatly entertained by a first-class West End revue and had laid her knitting down after the first number, so oil was poured on troubled waters and even Renée calmed down.

* * *

That week at Rawalpindi set the pace for the rest of the tour and an exhausting pace it certainly was with the thermometer steadily rising towards 100°F, with mess parties every night going on well into the small hours of the morning, and often also with long journeys to and from the neighbouring camps to which we went to perform. But it was exhilarating to know how much we were wanted, both professionally, as a show, and socially, as ourselves.

One of my most amusing memories of this week was of Renée at an evening party accompanied by two elderly colonels and a major, all of them having had one over the nine, being drilled in the boogie-woogie by a young subaltern who bossed them about as sternly as if he were a sergeant major with a line of raw recruits in front of him.

* * *

We left Pindi and travelled on to Kohart, one of the most attractive places on the tour with the bungalows built round a wide stretch of green grass, almost like an English village green. Here I was taken to see some Indian dancing, but found it disappointing, for the dancers had no technique at all — they just floated on and off the stage, vaguely waving their arms and smiling. Real Indian dancing is as much an art to be studied as ballet dancing and these dancers were clearly only amateurs.

* * *

A particularly pleasurable aspect of being in India was that we were frequently invited to full evening-dress dances. We had hardly ever worn evening dresses during the war in England and it was a joy to dance on the really lovely big floors of the clubs with a long frock floating round you. We went to a wonderful dance in Kohart in the club ballroom. There were banks of flowers and the long windows stood open to the night sky. The Gurkha band played waltz after waltz, with the most delicious lilt, and of course we were not allowed to sit down for a minute, with several fresh partners hurrying up to secure us after each dance.

Needless to say, we had it well drummed into us how spoilt women became in India because they were so much in the minority, but as we had come from a country where women nearly always outnumbered the men at any social function, it was delightfully refreshing to have the tables turned and I do not think any of us had our head turned too badly. Here, too, the attention, if ardent, was under control, and not the cave-man all-in tussle we had experienced at the casino near Phillipville.

* * *

Every day the heat increased and any exertion became more and more of an effort. None of us attempted to do anything during the middle part of the day unless we were forced to do otherwise. Captain Bull had promised us that by the end of June we should be up in the hills at Murray and we were soon panting for those hills. We fell onto our beds after our midday meal and lay there with next to nothing on under huge endlessly turning electric fans.

15

Tribal Territory: Travelling with an Armed Escort of Sikhs

Sometimes, though, we had to face the heat of the midday sun. One of the most exciting experiences of the tour was the journey through tribal territory in the Northwest Frontier Province.

For this adventure we had to leave early in the morning and travel in a long military convoy. All the women of the party had to travel together in a staff car; there were seven of us, eight before poor Jean hurt her back, and we were very squashed and naturally very warm. Behind us in the convoy came a lorry full of Sikhs to 'protect' us. They themselves looked so fierce with their beards, turbans, flashing eyes and glittering knives that we felt that they were just as likely to carry us off into the hills as any tribesmen.

The men of our company travelled much further back in the long procession. It was exciting to reach the notice at the roadside proclaiming 'TRIBAL TERRITORY'. Here, we all got out to stretch our legs and climbed up on the notice where Ivan took our photographs. But we were soon under way again, bumping along a winding road running between parched and barren-looking hills, and over dried-up rivers, where the salt lay thick on the riverbed.

In the army in India, Indian soldiers were responsible for all the maintenance work on army vehicles and, given that their talents clearly lay in other directions, one lorry after another in the convoy kept breaking down and holding up the whole procession until the trouble was put right. At each of these halts the captain of the Sikhs in the lorry load behind us would order his men to climb up the nearest hillside to scout around and about for danger. Once the repair had been seen to, the captain would order them back with a shrill whistle. With a face like a tiger and swearing violently, he would even throw stones at the poor unfortunate men who had in their zeal gone a little further in their search for tribesmen than the others had done and so were a little later in returning to base.

For hour after hour, we would sit grilling in our car, with our water bottles drunk dry and our throats parched with thirst, and still those army lorries kept breaking down one after the other and the convoy made to wait under the remorseless burning sun. We felt like screaming from the heat and boredom, and we even began to wish that the tribesmen would come swooping down from the hills and carry us off, for any change would have been better than none.

* * *

We eventually arrived at the other end without incident, however, and were taken off to private bungalows to rest before the show. Never have I been more thankful for a bath, even a tin one.

Before the performance started that evening, I wandered off across the gravel compound from the camp theatre to pick fresh flowers to wear in my hair and to pin onto the dress I would be wearing for *Love in a Mist*. There is, of course, a theatrical superstition against wearing real flowers on the stage, but I have never been bothered by superstitions, theatrical or otherwise. I had to go rather far to find any flowers and as I was turning back an Indian soldier suddenly grabbed hold of me. I screamed as loudly as I could, he loosened his hold, and I ran back to the theatre panting and breathless.

The others were horrified.

'You should report him at once, Catharine.'

'He should be well flogged.'

'He would be if the British officers knew.'

But I had no wish to get anyone flogged, British or Indian, and did not mention what had happened.

That was the nearest anyone got to being abducted on this trip, for the journey back was uneventful with a slightly lower percentage of breakdowns than we had when we were coming.

* * *

One Dicky Bull received us in Peshawar: he looked rather as if he expected to meet trouble and he certainly got it. He had to break the news that he had accepted luncheon invitations on our behalf from various regimental messes for every single day of the week — and this was over and above our after-the-show messes and the usual long treks out to neighbouring camps.

'Never mind,' he kept saying when we all complained about how exhausted we were feeling from the heat, 'this will be almost the last effort before you all go to the hills.'

Actually, despite being sorry about having to miss our siestas, we all enjoyed out time in Peshawar very much.

Some of the luncheons were very formal. The first one we went to, for example, was at a traditional Indian army mess and the Indian servants handling the beautiful silver dishes all wore tight white gloves and everyone else gave the impression of wearing them too. The atmosphere there was entirely different from that at most of the evening parties to which we were invited, where everyone drank, danced and made merry.

* * *

On one occasion the chief constable offered to escort us to the town's native quarter. He took us to the bazaar and guarded us carefully to ensure that we were not overcharged while we bought some of the lovely things being displayed for sale. I bought a lovely leaf green sari sprinkled with golden stars, which I afterwards had made up into an evening dress; a painted vase; and a couple of scarves, one pink, one green, worked with gold thread. The market square at Peshawar is remarkably fine and the crowd was colourful and animated. It upset me, however, to see the looks of hatred towards us on the people's faces. I noticed this a lot in India and it saddened me, for I myself felt nothing but friendliness towards them, but at the same time I realized how terrifying their hatred could be. I felt that I would not have gone through the Indian Mutiny for anything.

We had tea with the chief of police, native fashion, sitting on the floor surrounded by bazaar art and eating the most delicious sweetmeats.

* * *

An invitation to go up the Khyber Pass crowned the week. Several carloads, which the CO and his wife headed to give tone to the expedition, were going. Joy and I were assigned to a car with Peggy and Brian, a young officer with an artificial leg who was helping to organize our tour in the area. The others were insisting now that all the nervous ones must travel together on car drives along mountain roads so that we could all squeak out, 'go slower,' as often as we liked without annoying anyone else or making them nervous into the bargain. Brian promised to control the driver for us.

There was a flat run across the plain before we reached the foot of the mountains and the entrance to the pass. Then we began to climb, the narrow road twisting and turning on shelves of rock above deep cruel gorges below, then zigzagging higher and higher with the bare, rocky peaks towering above us.

There was another road that kept company with the new one we were on all the way up the pass. This was the old caravan route along which in former times long trails of camels had brought their burdens of silks and spices down into India from Persia and China.

The caravans had kept coming and going right up until the outbreak of the war, but the threat of a possible German invasion down the pass from Russia had turned the Khyber into a strongly fortified area. All the way up we passed concrete road defences ready to be rolled into position should the need arise. Brian told us that there were munition stores in the caves among the hills and that underground hospitals had been prepared in readiness.

When we reached the head of the pass, we all got out of the cars in which we were travelling to climb up a hill to have a good look at the view.

We were now right on the frontier of Afghanistan. Below lay a fertile valley stretching northwards with a deep blue river winding through it. Looking down on it from the wildness of the rocky mountains all around, I felt as if I were looking down on Alph, the sacred river of Kublai Khan.

Beyond the valley lay further hills, and through the distant mist we could just make out the hazy outline of the great Hindu Kush, beyond which, we were told, lay Russia.

It seemed incredible to be so near two vast countries, one of extreme heat and the other of extreme cold, here nearly touching one another.

* * *

One by one the different carloads turned up and when they had all arrived we left the hillside for the drive down into the valley to the little station of Lundi Kotel where we had been invited for lunch.

We had received three invitations — one from the commanding officer and two from other officers' messes — which meant that we had to split up; but first of all we gathered together for drinks on a green lawn under the trees.

It was a beautiful spot consisting of a walled-in garden completely surrounded by blue mountain ranges. Flamingos strutted across the lawn and flowers grew in profusion in the borders. After our hectic week, we longed to stay there and rest.

Our hosts entertained us as lavishly as usual at each of the three separate luncheons. Of course, when we compared notes afterwards, we all insisted that we had lunched at the venue with the best food and the most entertaining company.

As usual, it was a struggle to get away, but we explained that we had been invited to tea at the fort down at the other end of the pass and really must go.

* * *

The fort was a large, ominous prison-like erection. We were taken up onto the battlements to be shown the surrounding hills and glimpses of the Peshawar plain far down below. There was a magnificent view of the pass as well, cutting its way down between the mountains. We had pointed out to us the pickets on neighbouring hills where men had to remain on outpost duties — interminable those times seemed, they told us — in tiny isolated huts.

We had originally been invited for 'tea and a bathe in the pool', so we had come all prepared with our bathing suits, but in the meanwhile the commanding officer had decided that the sight of *memsahibs* bathing might be too exciting for the Indian troops and so he was very sorry but we would not be allowed to swim.

There was a party when we got back to Peshawar that evening. Being Sunday there was no show and the young women must not on any account be 'wasted'.

What a week!

16

Shah and Gulum Trouble: A Burglary and the Arrest of our Bearer

The next two places on our list, Risselpore and Camblepore, we had heard described by various officers as 'ghastly holes'. We were to give three shows in 'Rissy', and only one in Camblepore before going on up to Murray and the hills — those hills that were being dangled ahead of us like a carrot in front of a donkey.

We travelled by road from Peshawar. Everyone was nervous in the car that morning because the steering was obviously faulty and the driver merely looked over his shoulder and grinned whenever we missed something by a hair's breadth.

The country opened out onto a wide plain, vividly green and yellow in the sunshine, and after a while the blue mountains rose into view on the horizon. We crossed a rushing, deep blue river by a pontoon bridge and found ourselves driving up Rissy's main street. There were the usual bungalows, but they were not the same smart residential ones we had seen in Peshawar and Pindi — here there was more of a rough and ready barracks atmosphere about the place. But it certainly was not a 'hole' — there were the mountains in the distance and the wide river rushing past the compound, though I remember it being intensely hot there.

* * *

We were all to live in an empty bungalow and have our meals in the RAF mess. I dropped an enormous brick as soon as we had arrived and were taken to the mess for a late lunch. We were ushered into a large, panelled room, where the heads of wild animals looked imposingly down from the walls onto an even more imposing-looking very long and highly polished table spread for lunch.

'Oh,' I exclaimed, 'how typically Indian Army this all is!' One can imagine a Bateman cartoon of 'the girl in the RAF mess'.

With the exception of Peggy, with whom the RAF commanding officer had fallen head over heels in love, I do not think that any of us enjoyed our short stay in Risselpore very much.

* * *

First, there was trouble over the sleeping quarters. 'Feelings' within the company had risen with the thermometer and we were more or less divided into two camps by this time.

* * *

Second, there was trouble over one of the bearers. I have already mentioned our two bearers who travelled with the company. Besides looking after the costumes, Gulum attended to the two married couples, Ivan and Jack, while Shah looked after the rest of us — his 'six ladies'. We claimed that Shah was the better bearer. The others would not hear of anyone being superior to Gulum. Anyhow, they had both proved to be very satisfactory up to the present.

Then, at Risselpore, Frank and Joy had a locked case with money in it stolen from their room. It had been taken while we were at the theatre and while the two bearers and the *chokidar* (watchman) had been left to guard the bungalow.

Frank was deeply suspicious of Shah, and we felt resentful that our bearer, whom we had all grown to like, should be the one suspected. We insisted that the thief must have been someone who had gained entry from the back of the bungalow.

Our bearers were the only people who knew that Jack collected money from the bank each week with which to pay the hotel bills and the company's salaries and that he kept it in a locked suitcase in his room. The room that Jack (the pianist) and Connie occupied was next door to Frank and Joy's and it certainly looked as if someone who had been dropped a hint to go for the big fish had landed up with the smaller fry by mistake.

The officer suspected Shah, as did the Indian police when they turned up, and they took him off for further questioning, Shah with tears pouring down his face.

I remember how miserable we were that morning in the bungalow. Renée, Joan and I thinking of our poor Shah being beaten up by the police — we knew that this went on in order to make suspects talk — while Denny, one of the RAF officers, sat by explaining how one cannot trust any Indian servant and telling us how his bearer, who had served him faithfully for years, had emptied out a suitcase of his that had been packed full with stuff he had collected from all over India and had then filled it up with rubble before he, Denny, had left for England.

But we would not hear a word against Shah and were overjoyed when the police let him go and he returned to us. Months later, when we were to see Denny and the others again, they told us that the Indian police officer had been quite sure of Shah's guilt, but had let him off because the *memsahibs* had wanted it. Apparently, if a *sahib* or *mem-*

1. The author, Drury Lane, 1943

2. The *Marnix* at embarkation

3. Wedding in Cairo, 10 December 1943

4. ENSA entertainers preparing for the show

5. The author, Cairo, 1944

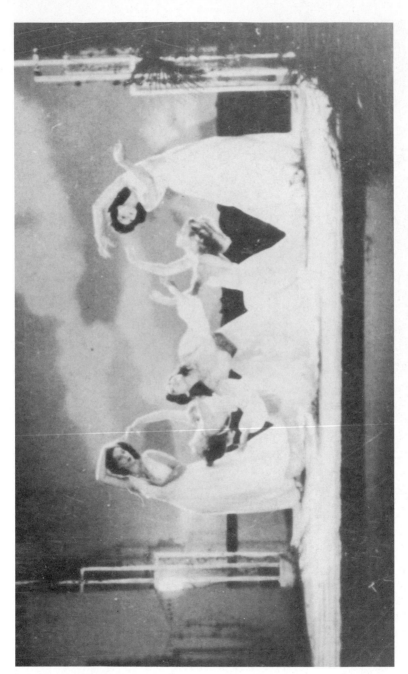

6. *Love in a Mist*, with (*left to right*) Joy, Jean, the author, Brenda and Peggy

7. Trip to the Northwest Frontier with *(left to right)* Indian bearers, Renée, Ivan, Joy, Frank, Joan, Brenda, Connie, Jack, the author and Sikh soldier

8. India, 1944. Front row (*left to right*): Brenda, the CO and the author. Second row: Officers and Jack (the pianist)

sahib wanted a servant to be found guilty, the police would see to it that he was, even if they themselves were unconvinced or even thought the opposite. Anyhow, Shah came back, dried his eyes and everything went all right for a time.

* * *

We gave two shows for the RAF in the tiny little crowded hall at 'Rissy' and one for the army. That night we found ourselves presented with lovely bouquets of flowers, which were handed up to the stage at the end of the performance.

We walked back into our RAF mess that night saying, 'look what the army have sent us!' For some reason, despite the flowers, we did not go to the army mess. There was a party with the RAF officers one night, with the sergeants on another, and on the third there was no invitation, which was a peaceful and lovely relief with everyone saying what a joy it would be to get an early night.

Somehow or other the evening finished up with Renée throwing a party in her room, to which everyone came, plus the two sergeants (Sandy and Barney), John, Denny and others from the mess and of course everyone stayed up even later than usual.

I sat on a bed and talked to Sandy. He was a nice boy, very young, sensitive and intelligent, and a clever arranger of music. He was not to be with us for long because ENSA wanted him back in Bombay in the music department.

He told me about having been a stretcher-bearer in Burma and about how much he had dreaded the nightmare sentry watches after darkness fell in the jungle when one man had to stay awake to rouse the rest should he hear the enemy coming. But the jungle is full of thousands of noises at night; any twig snapping might be a Jap creeping a little nearer or any noise in the bushes might be a body worming its way stealthily along and it was for the sentry to decide whether or not to wake the other men. All through those hours of inky darkness their lives were his responsibility.

* * *

At the RAF sergeants' mess party, we finished off the evening in the usual sergeants' mess style with a lot of hearty singing (censored versions with ladies present of course). I met there a young Don Juan among the sergeants. When I asked him if he had a girlfriend back home, he answered pleasantly, 'Well, I have four who write to me regularly, two others not quite so often. Anyhow, I'm pretty certain of getting at least two letters every day.' He went on to tell me that he was sick of being stuck here in 'Rissy' and wanted to be posted elsewhere.

'I've only to ask my CO's permission to marry an Indian girl and they'll post me soon enough!'

* * *

It was a beautiful drive to Camblepore. We left early so that we would have enough time to unpack and rest before the evening's performance. The following day we would move on again — up to Murray via Pindi — but when we got up there, we would have the whole weekend in which to rest. Murray is 6000 feet above sea level and we were told that we needed to get accustomed to the altitude and that it was considered dangerous for anyone to over exert themselves on first arriving up there.

The Camblepore road followed a wide, rushing, deep-blue river for a good deal of the way — the Kabul, the swiftest river in India. The snow-capped mountains across the plain showed up clearly that morning, dazzlingly white and blue in the sunlight, the plain so green and yellow. The loveliest point was the junction of the Kabul and the Indus, both wide, swift and unrestricted, rushing over the boulders and foaming into each other, with the snowy mountains, now much nearer, towering up behind. They were a magnificent range, white and glistening, soaring up into the sky; I felt that it was no wonder the Indian mythologists had chosen the Himalayas as a dwelling place for their immortals, for where else could immortals possibly dwell?

* * *

Camblepore was like a smaller Rissy lying in an even more remote stretch of the sun-baked plain, with mountains fringing the horizon.

The compound was very spread out and we were rather unhappy about the bungalow we had been given for the night. It seemed to be in a rather isolated position and we were all feeling a bit nervous since the recent burglary scare. However, the authorities promised to send along an army of *chokidar*s to guard us.

The nicest thing I remember about Camblepore was finding that there was mail waiting for us there, and nine letters among it were for me.

'That ought to keep her quiet for a bit,' said the others, who heard me enquiring after the post a bit too often.

* * *

We had a rather rough house that night. There were a lot of parachutists in the audience and these ones were as tough as they come and, of course, they just laughed at the ballet. Sometimes I felt embarrassed at coming up against that sort of reception on ENSA, but at other times it put me on my mettle and roused my fighting spirit.

Renée said that she found a difficult audience highly stimulating. She enjoyed imposing her will over a rowdy public, even if they were not really understanding or appreciating what was going on.

There was one terrible man in this audience with a hyena laugh that drowned the jokes, diverted the audience's attention away from the performance and exasperated the performers on the stage. That type of menace is equalled only by the 'front seat comedian' who makes his remarks in a loud voice for the benefit of his pals all around and, in the process, drowns out the performer's lines, diverts attention away from what is happening on stage and is generally a nuisance.

* * *

There was a dance in the hall for 'all ranks' after the show and little tables had been laid with drinks and refreshments outside a marquee. Someone carrying a goose was selling raffle tickets. Brenda was most indignant.

'A ballroom is no place for an animal,' she was announcing grimly in her deepest and fiercest voice.

Renée was asked to draw the raffle at the end and Connie won the goose, which she hastily returned for reraffling.

* * *

Once the dance was over, a group of Gurkha officers, or rather British officers in charge of Gurkha troops took us on to a party. I thought the soldier bearers in the mess, with their pork pie hats and long tight trousers, looked charming. The officers told us that they were wonderful fighters and had so much courage that once they had been given an order to go forward they would never dream of turning back. They showed us some of their knives, *kukri*s, with curved, cruelly sharp blades with which they could sever an animal's head from its body with a single blow. In due course, we all acquired *kukri*s to take home.

The Gurkha officers spoke with pride and affection about their men and, though more Gurkha officers got killed than in any other Indian regiment, they wore the 'black pips' with great pride. The men themselves were so tiny that their officers stood up like targets.

* * *

As a general rule, I found that the regular army officers in India thought the world of their Indian troops and that these feelings were reciprocated, but with civilians in the army for the duration of the war it was a different story. For the most part they hated India and they hated the Indians. Unlike the regulars, they had not chosen to come and were insufficiently interested in the men under them to feel any real sense of pride in their achievements or even any protective responsibility for them. The average British officer or soldier despised the Indians principally for their deceit and lack of truthfulness, a thing the British always find difficult to forgive, but they were quite insensitive to the racial differences that existed in standards and moral codes.

While I was in Egypt I sometimes wondered if the British and American soldiers ever paused to consider what the 'beastly wogs' they despised so much thought of their drunkenness and their free and easy manner with women. To walk in the park with your arm round a woman is highly offensive to a Muslim and of course strong drink is forbidden to them.

I once asked an officer in a West African regiment why he so much preferred African Negroes to Indians.

He gave me two answers straight off.

'Oh, you know where you are with them, you see,' and 'they treat you like gods.'

He could not have made himself clearer, I thought to myself — the British character abroad in a nutshell.

17

To the Hills: To Beautiful Murray on the Border of Kashmir

After a good many technical hitches of one description or another the following morning, we at last got going along the road to Rawalpindi. We passed by rice and wheat fields lying sweltering in the sun and occasional villages, which I longed to stop at and explore, for they looked so fascinating surrounded as they were by high walls with a domed temple rising up from the middle of the main square.

The trees by the wayside were heavy with rich vegetation. Bullock carts plodded along the middle of the road and we had to skirt round them when we came to them because the dust would rise up in clouds from the bullocks' feet.

* * *

On arriving back in Pindi, we went to the club for lunch where quite a few of our old friends had gathered to meet us. News certainly managed to get around in provincial India: they were surprisingly well informed about everything we had been doing and told us themselves about our trip up the Khyber and of the various parties we had been to at Kohart, Peshawar and Risselpore.

When lunch was over, some of us were keen to stay on for a while at the club, whereas others wanted to push straight on up to Murray. We were being sent up in three different cars and so Peggy, Ivan and I, who all felt we could not be there soon enough, went outside, selected what we thought looked like the nicest car and off we went. It certainly proved to have been the best choice, too, for both the other cars broke down on the way — in fact, the second car with Renée, Joan, Brenda and Jack in it, gave out completely and, after attempting to push it out of the ditch, they gave up and hitchhiked the rest of the way up by lorry.

* * *

But Ivan, Peggy and I sailed up the 6000 feet to Murray quite happily with our good steady driver.

What a lovely journey it was, too. The lower slopes, from where the heights above were completely hidden, were covered in thickly growing bushes. The road curled round a ravine above the deep bed of a dried-up river and then started to wind upwards and upwards. The country here rose in terraces of little patchwork fields. The mud huts, which had flat roofs, looked like fungi growing out of the hillside. Higher up still we came to pine woods, where Peggy and I hung out of the windows, delightedly breathing in the rich scent. How cool and fresh the air seemed and how tenderly green the woods after the heavy tropical greens on the plains below. There were the rocky beds of mountain streams, dried up now for the most part until the rains should come to give them back their life. We could trace their courses down the hillside and see where the water would come tumbling over the boulders between the pine trees above.

All the way up there were rest stations, which the army had used in peacetime when men used to be sent up to Murray on leave, marching in stages, all the way up.

123

We ourselves stopped at a village for tea, pulling up the car outside a little wooden shack.

It seemed strange suddenly to hear the 'Bluebells of Scotland' being piped to us while we sipped our tea. The piper was an old wrinkled-faced Indian squatting at the roadside. He told us that he had once served an officer in a Scottish regiment and that he had picked up the tune from his master. We finished our tea, gave the piper a few annas and went on again.

Each fresh curve of the mountain road brought wider and lovelier views and at last Murray itself came into sight, crowning the hilltop ahead, with red and green roofs appearing from among the trees. There was still a long way to go, for the road kept winding like a serpent, but at last we came to the first houses, wooden native dwellings, of this very straggling little hill town.

* * *

Here our taxi driver would take us no further because the road above was closed to motor traffic. Rikshaw *wallah*s, ragged, bare-footed and eager-eyed came hastening up. Peggy and I got into a rickshaw together; it was like a double-seated bath chair with three men pushing and two others pulling the long shaft in front. Ivan followed in another with our suitcases. The pathway up to the hotel was intensely steep and I must say that neither Peggy nor I enjoyed our rickshaw ride in the least. The men panted and gasped so much that we felt we would have much preferred to walk up.

We were told later that the men put on a good deal of the puffing and panting to win the ladies' sympathy and to get more *baksheesh*. It was also partly caused, though, by physical exertion at such a high altitude, which we were to discover for ourselves as soon as we started working.

Still, that ascent was undoubtedly a very stiff climb and we gave thankful glances at each other when they eventually put us down outside the hotel.

* * *

What a lovely hotel it was and in what a magnificent position! From the tea lawn in front of the main building the hillside made a sheer drop, so you felt as if you were hanging in space — it might have been the 'Terrace of God's House hung between heaven and earth' where the Blessed Damozel leaned out in Rossetti's poem: first, there was that great wide drop down into space and, further off, mountain peaks beyond mountain peaks rolled like the waves of a great sea to the horizon. Until that moment I had had no conception of how wonderful it felt to be so breathtakingly high up.

Jean, who had been in Murray since she had left the hospital at Rawalpindi, came hurrying out to meet us. And, despite the great bulky plaster jacket in which her body was encased and which she would have to wear until the bones of her back were set, she was looking very well. Her cheeks were rosy from the mountain air and she was delighted to be seeing us all again.

We two were to share a room, as we had done before, and Jean took me off to the annexe behind the hotel to show it to me.

A steep flight of wooden steps led up to a little green-roofed chalet. We had our own front door leading into a tiny sitting room ten feet square with the bedroom beyond. The annexe spread itself out in other chalets beneath the pine trees. From their branches hung tiny electric light bulbs to guide people to their rooms at night.

From this side of the hotel, the view was even lovelier to my mind, for here we could look across the intervening valley to rich pine-covered slopes, with — further up the ravine — the first snowy peaks of the Kashmir Mountains. I found that I could sit for hours at the window of our little sitting room, drinking in the view of the pine trees, the mountains, the fresh cool air and the peace.

We lived like lords at the hotel and only wished that our families back in England could have shared some of the enormous and delicious meals we were served. Poor Jean, she was admittedly fond of her food, but there was no room inside her plaster jacket for large meals. What upset her most, though, about wearing the jacket was that it made her look pregnant. Murray was full of pregnant women and she had no wedding ring.

* * *

We were given the weekend off and our first three performances on the Monday, Tuesday and Wednesday were to take place at a hall in the town, so we had plenty of time to explore the neighbourhood and enjoy the hotel garden.

We went on shopping expeditions up the steep main street — called the Mall of course, even here — where the shops were stocked full of Kashmiri goods, including woodcarvings, papier-mâché work, embroidery and furs. The latter were very reasonably priced, but we were warned to ensure that the skins had been properly cured before we bought them.

I got myself an embroidered Kashmiri wool dressing gown and two nightdresses, besides quite a few presents to take home.

* * *

Down below the Mall and 'out of bounds' to HM forces lay the native market. We could look down on it, though, from a terrace leading off the Mall and descending into narrow cobbled streets that dropped down the steep incline; lined with open-fronted shops these streets thronged with Indians who, judging from the variety of costumes they wore, presumably came from a number of different races.

I stood there on the terrace for a long time, very early on Sunday morning, before going to the service at the little English church, and watched the life below — the people coming to wash themselves under the pump and to fill up their pitchers. Below the wooden walls of the houses, the hillside dropped away in terraces of tiny fields, and the hills across the valley were cut up in the same way, except where the pinewoods clustered thickly. Miles away, somewhere beneath in a soft blue haze, lay the plains.

* * *

One day a couple of RAF officers, whom we had first met in Peshawar, took Brenda, Joy and me riding on a course. Riding in Murray consisted of sitting on horseback and going to see the view, for the roads were too steep to do much more than walk along them and, in any case, not that many of us could really ride. But it was the best way to see the country.

We climbed up to Kashmir Point, the road winding up through fir trees of a colossal height until we came out into the open at the crest of the hill, from where the full view of the snow range — the Kashmir mountains — burst upon us. How we longed to go there! We decided that we must ask for a leave to be spent in Kashmir.

* * *

Our audiences in Murray were nearly all to consist of troops on leave. We were to give three shows in the town and three at various camps round about, with the last on the list being an American leave camp. The next week we were to go away to a place called Abbatobad, described to us as a semi-hill station, and return to Murray the week following to play to the fresh batches of men, who by that time would have arrived on leave and changed places with our previous audiences.

Altogether it was a nice programme, though it was certainly disappointing to find that dancing in that rarefied mountain air, which we had hoped to find such a relief, was in fact far more exhausting than it had been in the heat of the plains below. We gasped for air and at times became quite giddy. I dreaded my circle of pirouettes at the finish of my dance, feeling as if I would land up over the floodlights every time. Frank, too, found singing more of an effort — he had to draw two breaths, he told us, where he would normally have drawn only one.

There were no 'messes' to follow the first three performances at the hall in the town. It was very pleasant walking back to the hotel in the evening and joining Jean in our little chalet.

* * *

One night, a sudden thundering on the iron roof overhead gave us quite a shock, and we rushed to the window to catch sight of a little long-tailed marmoset monkey leap through the air from the roof above us to the trunk of a pine tree 15 feet away.

After that we often heard the marmosets and always went to the window to watch with amazement the little creatures soaring through the air from tree trunk to tree trunk: the distances they could leap seemed quite incredible.

Always after dark we would hear the jackals baying from the distant hills across the valley. Jean thought it was a horrible sound, but to me it had an eerie fascination.

* * *

On the Wednesday we did an early show and then Renée,

To the Hills: To Beautiful Murray on the Border of Kashmir

Joan, Brenda, Peggy and I went off to the local cinema, which, we were told, was always so many miles behind the times, that quite recently Mr Chamberlain and his umbrella had appeared on the newsreel.

We all sat in a row with our feet up on the seats in front and Renée remarked: 'I wonder what some of the chaps we have been meeting all this time would say if they could see us five sitting here on our own like this?'

* * *

The next day we drove to a camp situated on a hilltop, which could be seen from Murray, though it took some time to get there by road.

Here, we had to rig up our portable stage in the open air and the audience sat on chairs in front, squatted on the grass, or swarmed up the banks behind. We changed in tents, one for the men, one for the women. We were extremely squashed and had no chairs and no mirrors — in fact the whole thing was a bit of a picnic.

When the show over, we were taken off to dinner at the officers' mess, and then outside into the night to where the men were roasting a pig, whole, over a bonfire, and swilling down beer. We separated and each joined a table, getting a terrific welcome as we sat down among them all. Jack (our pianist) went to the piano, and Frank led them off in a sing-song.

It was an evening I shall always remember, the freshness of the night air on that mountain, the crackling bonfire with the blackened pig slowly turning on its spit in the middle, and the crowd of young soldiers sitting round with their mugs of beer, joining in song after song, until Frank's throat was hoarse and Jack's fingers could play no more.

* * *

The following night we took the show to a convalescent camp. There was an invitation to the mess for dinner afterwards and then a further one to an 'all-ranks' dance. Some of us stayed for the dance and others went on home. The latter included Peggy and Brenda, both of whom were feeling tired and not very well, so without them and Jean we were fewer women than ever to provide partners for all the men and got even more danced off our feet than usual. At 'all-ranks' dances we invariably came up against the same barrier of suspicion.

'Oh you ENSA girls, you've no use for anyone but the officers.'

Fortunately, I always had an answer for this sort of remark.

'Well, I married a lance corporal,' I would say and would become popular at once.

18

Over the Horse's Head and to Hospital

We got back very late that night, but had to be ready the following day after an early lunch to be fetched by the Americans and taken over to their camp about twenty-five miles away, along what we had been warned was a simply terrifying mountain road. In fact, Peggy, Joy, Connie and I had been teased about this forthcoming journey all through the week.

The road was so narrow that it was only open to motor traffic travelling one way in the morning and the other way in the afternoon. However, because of the extreme danger of travelling along there at all after dark, we were to spend the night at the camp and come back the following day. Fortunately, by this time we were becoming more familiar with these mountain roads and getting used to looking down from the car windows over sheer drops of several thousands of feet and to turning hairpin bends that made you feel as if you were going clean over into space. Luckily, too, we had a very steady American driver with us.

Peggy, Connie, Joy and I in the one car together did not mind the journey as much as we had anticipated. The scenery was so exquisitely beautiful, every curve of the road bringing fresh aspects of the sky, then of the mountains, from the thickly wooded crests to the patchwork terraced slopes below, with the valleys lying somewhere far beyond in the hazy distance. Each hill that we encircled swung us nearer into view of the snow-covered Kashmir ranges, entrancingly and dazzlingly white, that seemed to tower up higher and higher as we approached.

A particularly nasty moment occurred on the drive when we were going up an especially steep slope. The Indian driver of a large lorry in front of us suddenly decided to change gear, with the result that his vehicle started to run backwards on top of us. Our driver kept a perfectly cool head, backing our car while at the same time yelling to the car behind us to do the same. Luckily, the Indian managed to get his lorry under control again, but Connie and Peggy admitted that they had already marked out which trees they were going to cling to down below when the car went overboard and, as for me sitting on the inside, I had my door open and my hand on the handle, ready to spring out onto the bank the next minute.

Passing other vehicles on the road was quite impossible except at special places. We dreaded getting behind these great lumbering uncertain lorries, or the rattletraps of buses, crowded to the roof with natives, blowing out fumes and making a noise like Waterloo station. How anyone dared to trust themselves in the things I really do not know.

* * *

When we eventually arrived at the camp — red-roofed huts among the pinewoods — the young American sergeant in a cowboy hat who met us approached me with:

'Say, are you Catharine Marks the ballet dancer?'

Feeling somewhat honoured, I said that I was and wondered what was coming next.

'Your pals, who have just arrived, tell me that you are the letter writer of the company and I am looking for someone who would care to correspond with me.'

'Well, I'm afraid it takes me all my time writing to my husband,' I said hastily, thinking that here I had a sufficiently dampening excuse. But Young America was not to be put off so easily.

'Oh that's nothing,' he snorted, 'I write my fiancée every day, but [with vigour] I'd write anyone else who's woman enough to write to me.'

He did not mention whether or not his fiancée might have been woman enough to object.

* * *

A slim, dark and attractive young woman from the Red Cross showed us to our sleeping quarters, which were in long wooden huts, and left us to unpack and rest for a while before coming down to the mess for an early American supper. It was quite a treat to have glasses of milk with the meal, the Americans at this camp having their own cows especially laid on.

Then they piled us into jeeps and jogged us down a crazily steep cart track to the theatre; coming down the side of one of the Pyramids in a jeep could not have been more alarming.

* * *

While making-up and getting dressed, we feverishly discussed what lines we could change in the show to make the humour more comprehensible to our American audience — we had not realized before pulling things to bits that practically every joke bore some reference to England or to something typically English.

Well, they applauded the show cordially and expressed their appreciation afterwards but, despite all our efforts, they did not laugh very much and we felt that the show had been somewhat less successful than usual.

After the 'Star Spangled Banner' had been played and we had packed up our things, a group of sergeants escorted us to a party that was being held in one of the huts. We squeezed into the few chairs that were available, or perched on the arms or sat on the floor, while we drank beer out of cans and threw the empties across the room into the fireplace. Someone had brought a banjo along and everyone sang American and British songs as the heap of beer cans in the fireplace rose higher and higher.

The next morning they saw us off and, with their usual American generosity, they showered us with cartons of Camel cigarettes and chocolates.

* * *

There was only one incident on the way back, which was at a sudden bend in the road when we came upon a man leading two heavily laden mules. In passing, although we barely touched the bulging pack strapped onto the back of one of them, the animal started to plunge and rear on the narrow road and the muleteer had to use all his strength to pull it back from the edge of the precipice. He was probably cursing us heartily at the same time.

There was a mountain route to Abbatobad, our next date, but Dicky Bull, who was still arranging the tour and turning up every now and again to see how everything was going, thought we might have had enough of mountain roads by this time and had arranged for us to go across the plains. This meant going down into Pindi and then up again to Abbatobad, which was a longer distance in mileage though shorter in time.

* * *

We left Murray early to get through as much of the journey as possible before it grew too hot, and were down in Pindi by eleven o'clock, stopping for drinks at Flashman's and then pushing straight on again.

This time Renée, Joan, Peggy and I were in a car together, with Peggy in front. After a while, she politely suggested to the Indian driver that he should sing us a song. This was a fatal suggestion. The song, which we all applauded and said was *tiki*, was followed up by a continuous outpouring of melody all the way to Abbatobad, which to our ears was as monotonous as the wail of a kitten shut up in a basket.

We tried to break the stream by giving him a song of our own, 'Where the Bee Sucks', which we all trilled together in fairy voices. Our driver said it was *tiki* and immediately gave us another of his own compositions in return.

He would only break off his song to shout furiously at the other drivers we passed on the road. Admittedly, he was quite a good driver and most of the others were rotten, but it was all we could do to prevent him turning in at the military police to report half the cars on the road.

* * *

We were not to stay in Abbatobad itself, but at a settlement a couple of miles further on, an unattractive looking place consisting of corrugated-iron-roofed bungalows and huts gathered together in a dip between the hills. The population was almost entirely military. There were a good many Gurkhas stationed there with their families who had dainty, pretty little bright-eyed wives and fascinatingly sweet children.

We were dispersed to sleeping quarters at various bungalows, though for meals we were to meet at the all-ranks' club.

I remember my sleeping quarters chiefly because of all the insects; there were swarms of them. I would spend hours before I could get to sleep killing the bugs in the bed, then going all over the floor with a slipper after the gigantic red cockroaches that made a horrible squelch when squashed, and finally chasing the mosquitoes up and down the walls, throwing at them anything I could lay hands on in my exasperation.

* * *

The performances took place in a quite sizeable, long, low garrison theatre built of wood. It had one of the smoothest and largest stages we had yet come across and, for once, I was able to enjoy the ballet instead of feeling frustrated.

We went on afterward to a Gurkha officers' mess where there was the usual singing of old favourites (the old favourites thought to be suitable when ladies were present) such as 'My Brother Sylvert' and 'Old King Cole'.

It was distressing to see the extreme youth of most of the officers present, such young first and second lieutenants, because we knew that the regiment was being ordered up into Burma very soon.

* * *

Brenda was making an arrangement with one of them, a red-haired youth of about twenty-two, by no means one of the youngest, for some riding for us the following day. He promised to bring round three horses in the afternoon and Brenda suggested that Joy and I should come too.

We told him that we were beginners — Brenda was in fact much more experienced than either Joy or me — and he promised to bring very nice quiet horses. I must admit to feeling a little nervous when I saw the size of them the next day, though our escort Roy assured us that they were quite gentle.

This was the third time I had gone riding in India, the other occasions being once in Peshawar and once in Murray, both of which I had much enjoyed. The only prior experience I had had was nearly ten years previously on a friend's pony in the country when I was a ballet student, and I had kept dismounting at gates to do pliés in an attempt to counteract whatever harm I was doing to myself by pressing my knees in instead of out.

I think that this was only Joy's second ride.

We first just walked the horses up and down the gravel lanes. Roy said the surface was far too rough for the horses' hooves to risk trotting on, but that he would take us into a field where we could have a nice canter round.

We turned out of the hot dusty lane into a wide-open field, and our three horses just threw up their heads and bolted.

I had never galloped before in my life, and I must say that, terrified as I was, it was a wonderful sensation to be flying over the ground at that speed, the horse's hooves thundering underneath me, passing first Brenda's horse, then Joy's and then just letting go into one mighty rush across the whole length of the field to the far distant corner. Of course, I tugged frantically at the reins, but my quiet gentle horse deemed so suitable for a beginner (we learnt afterwards that these were full-blooded war horses trained to go at a terrific speed) took no more notice of me than if I had been a fly sitting on its back. The last thing I could remember was seeing a road ahead at the end of the field with a ditch in between and thinking:

'Now this will be the end' — and it was.

* * *

When I came round I found myself lying on a slab in the military hospital with my hair being cut off in chunks from the back of my head. The doctor told me afterwards that I had made far more fuss over losing my hair than over the wound in my scalp that they were about to stitch together.

There was a fiery hotness at the back of my head, a shooting pain in one leg and a blurred jumble of faces —

Brenda's familiar and reassuring and the nurse's with the scissors — and then I lost consciousness again to be whirled off into the wildest and most vivid dreams.

The next morning the company all trooped in to see me and to say goodbye because they were going back to Murray that day. Joy and Brenda were both with them. The latter had purposely rolled off her horse as soon as it had started to bolt. She was covered in bruises from the hardness of the sun-baked Indian ground and had wrenched her foot, which was to keep her out of the show for a week. Joy had got off scot-free because, with Roy's help, she had been able to rein in her horse before it threw her.

They told me that the doctor had said I would be up again in three weeks' time to join them on the way up to Kashmir for our eagerly awaited leave.

I would be missing the return to Murray and the 'mystery date' that was to follow. It had been kept a strict secret where we would be going, though most of us had already guessed, and we were very excited about it. Disappointed though I felt over missing all that, as long as I could join them for the week in Kashmir I did not mind too much. It was such a relief to know that I had not broken any bones, my leg had only been wrenched at the socket and, although the doctor came in the next morning callously joking about measuring me up for a wig, the nurse reassured me later that they had only had to cut off my hair over a patch at the back, and that I should be able to arrange the rest of my hair to cover it.

19

Left Behind: The Company Goes on to Razmak

When the company went back to Murray, I was left behind in the Abbatobad hospital. I think it was the noisiest hospital you could possibly imagine. On the other side of the road there was a shooting range, which the army seemed to keep in constant use throughout the day. Down the corridor from me a couple of newborn babies yelled their heads off, while a third arrival was to be expected in the very near future to judge from the shrieks of 'I can't bear it nurse' from the prospective mother. Then there was a Gurkha band that used to come round and play outside the hospital in the afternoons to cheer up the patients. But the limit of endurance was reached when workmen started to pull down a wall right outside my ground-floor window.

With a splitting headache from the concussion and being forbidden to read or use my eyes in any way, which might have taken my mind off the banging outside, I could do nothing but roll on the bed in torture. Eventually, the nurse came in and found me with tears streaming down onto the pillow and persuaded the sister in charge to change her attitude of 'Oh, they'll have finished the job in a few days' and let me be moved to another wing.

I was kept in bed solidly for three weeks. Every morning I

would have a fight with the doctor who was falling back on his promise to let me go to Kashmir with the others. He had not realized, he said, that they were to go for only one week and that I must have a whole month's convalescence before working again in the heat.

I was horrified at at the idea of having come out to India to do a six-month tour with a show and then having to be out of it for two months out of the six. It was only when the doctor told me that I might land up with headaches for the rest of my life that I submitted and the daily fights came to an end.

* * *

There had been accidents in several of the companies lately and the office in Bombay was beginning to get exasperated with them. Apart from the accident to the singer of one show — who while taking her bow had stepped backwards off the edge of the platform, crashing through the back curtains and down the drop behind — all the other accidents had taken place well out of office hours. These were Jean's injury to her spine through diving, my riding disaster and an accident to a woman in Freddy Pain's company who, we heard, was in hospital after having been mauled by an officer's pet tiger.

In fact, I was told that ENSA had issued a new ruling that in future anyone unable to work through activities such as diving, falling off horses or getting mauled by tigers would receive no salary until they were back in their shows again. I felt it rather hard that having risked my neck behind Indian drivers on mountain roads, going twice through tribal territory, not to mention the dive-bombing on the way out and our unescorted trip across the Indian Ocean, here I was landed up in hospital after what had been unmistakably a case of taking my own amusement.

* * *

John Gonella, who was the staff captain responsible for our company while the show was in Abbatobad, could not have been a better friend to me during the entire period in which I was in hospital. He used to come in to see me every day to keep me company and would also bring me anything he thought I might want.

The most welcome thing he brought me was a portable gramophone, which proved to be the greatest boon once the headaches had lifted, for I was forbidden to read for some time and got very bored. Outwardly, he was a little reserved, but underneath it all John Gonella had a very likeable character with a good sense of humour. Certainly his friendship made all the difference to my time in hospital.

* * *

Another visitor I had who used to amuse me very much, though quite unconsciously, was a young subaltern from the Gurkha mess we had gone to after the first performance. Nineteen years old, with light curly hair and a very boyish face, he would sit on the edge of the bed and come out with such remarks as:

'You know, curiously enough, I have had very little experience of women really.'

He was obviously intending to have more. He confided to me his feelings for a nurse in another wing of the hospital.

'But she has gone and got engaged to a beastly major' — with scornful emphasis on the last word — 'and where do you think he took her to propose? He took her out onto our shooting ground at night when the sky was full of lots of pretty lights. If I had known they were there, I would have shot them both dead.'

* * *

A third visitor was Roy, our riding master, who came in looking highly embarrassed and guilty. He asked me if there was anything he could do for me or get me from the town. Poor Roy, he had had a bad shock and a severe dressing down from his commanding officer. And a few days later he was to break his arm falling off a horse of his own.

John Gonella told me that he would not have taken a woman out on one of those horses, even with a leading rein.

* * *

Meanwhile, the company had finished its return week at Murray and was preparing for the bonne-bouche of the Northwest Frontier tour, the trip to this mysterious place, which was being kept such a dead secret but which everybody had already correctly guessed was Razmak, situated right up in the mountains on the frontier and known as the largest monastery in the world; no woman had ever been allowed in there before. Dicky Bull had had a hard tussle with the military authorities to get permission for our company to go up, but was determined to achieve it, even if old Indian army colonels did snort over the news of 'women in Razmak' from the clubroom armchairs.

* * *

I heard enthusiastic accounts of the ten days there from the company, though not very detailed descriptions, more sighs of 'it was all marvellous, you should have been there Catharine' than anything else, but I shall do my best to describe things at second hand.

They were first flown over a part of the tribal territory and then taken on by road with a heavily armed escort. Once they arrived at Razmak itself, the reception they got was quite overwhelming, with troops lining the streets, bands playing and terrific cheering from all sides. One or two of the women openly wept with emotion. They all had to get out of the cars in which they were travelling to imprint their footmarks in a large patch of wet cement to commemorate being the first women to set foot in such an exclusively masculine stronghold.

A beautiful stage had been specially built for the company's visit, the nicest we had worked on anywhere, they all said, with by far the best lighting system, not quite Strand Electric, but at any rate variable with spots and colours. Of course there were the gayest parties every night after the show at the many messes in the town, and they all rarely got to bed before four or five in the morning.

The thing I most regretted having missed was the Petains' display of dancing. Brenda said they were magnificent and described how they worked themselves up into the wildest abandonment, dancing at tremendous speed with the most astonishing leaps into the air and whirling of swords.

All the men in the company were taken to dinner with one of the Petain chiefs. It was not thought advisable for the ladies to go because the Petains were considered quite capable of inviting you to dinner one day and shelling your roof the next, so they could not be trusted too far. The women came back from Razmak, however, with very fine Petain daggers as presents and they brought a couple of extra ones for the two of us who had missed it all, namely Jean and me.

The ten days finished up with the hanging of a special ENSA shield, 'The Fair Sex', beside the colours of all the regiments that had ever been stationed in Razmak.

* * *

Meanwhile, Captain Gonella had promised me a slice of excitement to help make up for all that I was missing up at Razmak. This was in the shape of General Auchinleck (the 'Auk') who was coming round on a tour of inspection and was to visit the hospital. John promised to arrange for a photograph to be taken with me in his august company. As he was the staff officer, it was Captain Gonella's job to see to the 'Auk's' comfort and convenience while he was on his tour of inspection. He had already mentioned me during the course of entertaining the great man and had told him the story of the three ENSA women and their riding adventure and of how I had described ourselves as 'complete beginners except Brenda who had more experience because she owned her own jodhpurs'. John never let me forget that and the 'Auk' seemed to find it funny too.

Everybody at the hospital was in a flutter on the day of the visit. The sisters, all looking their sprucest, would come bustling in every other minute to see that everything was tidy and in order. The senior sister, a tubby little Anglo-Indian came in, whisked off one of my vases of flowers to put in the sisters' room, where the 'Auk' was to have his tea, and I never saw them again.

* * *

The great man arrived, big, sunburnt and with rows of shining medals. We shook hands, he asked how I was, the cameras clicked and that was that. Then he was whisked off to the tea prepared in the sisters' room, where, the senior sister told me afterwards, the younger ones had behaved disgracefully, hanging round the general in doting admiration and cooing for favours. Some asked him to have them posted elsewhere to be nearer a fiancé here or a boyfriend there. The general obviously enjoyed all the attention and promised to give them whatever they asked for.

* * *

It was not long after this that I began to get up for a little each day.

'One always knows when a woman is getting better,' said the doctor, coming in while I was trying to arrange my hair over the shaved patch at the back, 'she starts to take an interest in her appearance again.'

* * *

I had received by now two or three letters from members of the company, which hinted at the glories of Razmak but deplored the fact that the Kashmir leave had been 'mucked up' and that they would be going back to Murray again to spend their free week there. I also heard through Ivan that I was to spend my month's convalescence up there too, with Jean at a 'ladies rest home', which did not sound wildly inviting. I should be going up to Murray just as the rest of the company were leaving, for the doctor had now decided to keep me on for a fourth week in hospital. We hoped to arrange, however, that I should meet them all for lunch in Pindi. They would be coming down to catch the train for Calcutta, where the show was booked for the whole of July.

I cannot say that I felt very sorry at the prospect of spending a month in the hills instead of in the sweltering city I had always connected in my mind with the 'Black Hole', much as I hated the thought of the show going on without me.

* * *

We had been told that, now that the monsoon had broken, Calcutta would not be quite as bad as we had heard it would be. Freddy Pain's company, which had been working in Bengal throughout May and June, had had the worst of the heat. Its members had so much illness later on that they all had to be sent to Darjeeling for a time to recuperate and the show had to be taken off the road. Our company was to play at other places in Bengal after the season at the Besa Theatre in Calcutta, but to everyone's disappointment we were not to go up to Assam and Burma. With all the transport difficulties and because we had a lot of costume boxes, the company was considered too large to take right forward.

* * *

Noel Coward had just been to Burma, and so had Stainless Stephen and Elsie and Doris Waters. Vera Lynn was leaving for England after having completed a very strenuous, but unfortunately not a very extensive, tour. Although she had worked amazingly hard, giving as many as six shows a day in the tremendous heat, it had been impossible for her in the six weeks available to her to reach all the camps in which the men were living. It was the same story with Gracie Fields's visits to the Eighth Army in Italy; not everyone was able to see the star and those who did not felt bitter about it.

I also heard afterwards from soldiers who had been up in Burma that they would have preferred to see Miss Lynn in a feminine fluffy evening gown rather than in slacks. An audience never thinks of the practical difficulties the performers have to face, such as how is one supposed to iron feminine fluffy dresses in the wilds of Burma. They expect a certain standard, and it is a good thing that they do, though how often a pianist longs to explain in a loud voice that he cannot play the music properly with the pages blowing all over the place in the open air, a singer to explain that his voice is getting completely lost in the vastness of hangars, or again in the wind, or for a dancer to explain that her pirouettes cannot come off properly when at every step she keeps catching her toe in the irregularities of the stage.

Sickness, too, is a thing for which the artiste can never expect any excuse. How is the audience to know that a performer has a sore throat or blisters on her toes? Vera Lynn was to go down with malaria as soon as she arrived home in England, an illness that often develops after a change of climate.

* * *

On my last day in hospital, the woman doctor gave John permission to take me to a party at the club.

She agreed to my going so long as I did not swim or dance. I had no evening dress with me, so John went off and borrowed one from a friend of his, making a very good choice; it was a pretty cotton gown in a pink and black tartan. Nearly all the women in India seemed to wear cotton evening dresses because a silk or satin one could so easily be ruined by one night's sweat.

I enjoyed slipping on the dress and piling up my hair on top.

I do not know whether or not the people at the party were typical of British society in India at that time, but certainly our dressing room conversations were modest and demure compared with theirs, and a lot more amusing. The men, all army types, all more or less sozzled, were to become more so as the evening wore on. Their lady friends, most of whom were grass widows with husbands in Burma, were hard-boiled and racy. Their talk centred largely on drink, on who had drunk what, when, and how much.

I had been forbidden to touch any alcohol for two months, so I sat there feeling very chilly and out of things. There was, however, a delightful Gurkha band in the ballroom. Of course they could not play 'swing', but they had a wonderful rhythm of their own.

I was enchanted when one small man stood up and sang 'White Christmas'. One could not distinguish a single word, but I have never heard it sound so pleasant before or since.

I could not resist getting up for a couple of slow dances with John, only to find that the floor was full of sisters from the hospital who wagged their heads and shook their fingers at me.

20

Flight to Calcutta: After Convalescing in Murray I Rejoin the Show

The temperature at Rawalpindi at this time was as high as 115°F. The atmosphere was stifling when, after leaving the hospital, we arrived at noon the following day at Flashman's Hotel. I collapsed onto a sofa under the fan in Dicky Bull's sitting room and stayed there until the company turned up. They arrived with a lot of kind enquiries about how I was feeling and Jack Murray anxiously asked after the welfare of the horse.

* * *

Only three of them had spent their leave in our lovely Cecil Hotel in Murray, the others having been fixed up at various little hotels in the town, some of them apparently most disagreeable. They were all storming against Donald, whom they thought might have arranged things a bit better. Of course, when I arrived in Murray I heard Donald's side of the story about how impossible the company members had been when they had come up on leave.

I was sorry not see Renée and Joan among them, but they had flown to Calcutta for their leave, for Renée to meet the famous colonel about whom we had heard so much.

Flight to Calcutta: After Convalescing in Murray

* * *

I hated saying goodbye to them when they went off to catch the four o'clock train, groaning at the thought of the three-day journey across India. Poor wretches, they did not know what they were in for, either. Their coach was to get unhitched one night with the result that they got shunted onto another line and the journey was to take five days instead of the expected three. Then, on top of the heat, the dirt and the tedium, they had no food because they had become separated from the restaurant car and from the van containing their emergency rations. They had to live on mangoes bought on the station platforms, a dish that may sound quite pleasant but certainly does not have the happiest effect when taken in surfeit in a country like India.

* * *

I found a very depressed Jean waiting for me at the Ladies' Rest Home. She was still encased in her plaster jacket and feeling thoroughly fed up and miserable. For myself, though, my spirits soared at the sight of the Ladies' Rest Home. Dreary as the name sounded, it was in fact a delightful spot perched up on the highest point above Murray, a pleasant enough house surrounded by lawns and giant pine trees, with the hillside dropping away into the woods on all sides and cool refreshing views of the Kashmir mountains from the many windows.

I must admit that my month's convalescence up there in the hills was my most pleasant memory of India. The peace, solitude and beauty of the Himalayas completely over-powered me and I felt that I would like to spend the rest of my life there. Jean, however, was aching to get back into the show again, shunning any sociability because of the plaster jacket and moping over her enforced idleness.

We had not been there more than a week when two

149

officers came knocking at the front door. They had seen the magic word 'ladies' on the gatepost and had come in to ask for drinks of water. They might at least have thought up a better excuse. So, after that I had invitations to the club on several evenings in the week, though Jean was too self-conscious to come with me. Those were pleasant informal little parties and I enjoyed them, though what I liked best was the ride home in a rickshaw open to the night sky, with the wonderful giant fir trees on either side of the road towering up to the stars, the soft rhythmic panting of the bearers close at hand and in the distance the call of the jackals. My companion was pleasant, but fortunately unob-trusive.

I remember arriving back at the rest home one evening to find the veranda covered in cockroaches lying on their backs and weakly kicking their legs in the air. Being a good Hindu, the *chokidar* (night watchman) could not take life so was unable to kill them, but because they worried him by walk-ing over his legs he was forced to put them out of action by some other means.

* * *

My month was up and Dicky Bull came to take me back to Rawalpindi, where he was to put me on an aeroplane to fly across India to rejoin the company. Jean had still another two weeks to wait and I left her in tears.

I did the flight in two stages, stopping a night in Delhi on the way. The first day's trip in a small four-seater aeroplane was quite pleasant, the second day's in a larger Dakota flying low I found most objectionable and was very sick. I took advantage of being the only woman on board to ask the pilot to fly higher, which he obligingly did.

It was tantalizing to stop for only one night in Delhi, and I looked in vain for the Taj Mahal from the air, though the aerial view of Delhi was magnificent. New Delhi I found disappointing. Here were 'the Mall' again and the suburban-looking bungalows. Of Old Delhi I caught only a mere glimpse on my way to the hotel where I was to spend the night.

* * *

Arriving in Calcutta reminded me of the arrival in Cairo after dark, with the long straight course of the runway lighted up and searchlights to guide us in.

I found Brenda at the Grand Hotel and shared a room with her that night. The rest of the company, having finished their season at the Besa Theatre, had gone on to Ranchi from where I was to follow them the next day. Poor Brenda had chest trouble and was being kept under observation by the doctor. Working in the damp heat of a Bengal summer had been too much for her. Always pale, she now looked ashen and painfully thin.

I cannot say that I liked the Grand Hotel and Brenda positively loathed it. It was rather like a vast railway station on an August bank holiday, crowded, noisy and airless, with a never-ceasing din. With the humidity of the atmosphere, everything seemed damp and sticky to the touch and horrible things came crawling out of the waste pipes in the bathrooms. I was glad to leave for Ranchi the next day .

A most trying incident took place on the journey. The ENSA corporal who took me to the train had my suitcase, containing a good many things I had collected in India to take home as presents, put on the back of an open lorry and, not surprisingly, when we arrived at the station the suitcase was not there and I never saw it again.

Calcutta station appalled me. It was as crowded as the Grand Hotel, but this time with beggars and down-and-outs in the most wretched states of destitution and disease just lying about everywhere. It was distressing enough to see them in the streets, pestering for annas outside the Grand

Hotel, holding out withered arms or half starved babies, but here they just lay hopelessly, almost as if they were piled up for the dustcart.

* * *

Ranchi was a straggling little town and the hotel in which the company was staying was about a mile from the shopping centre. Open rice fields all around were looking very fresh and green from the rains, which had now well and truly broken. The hotel consisted of a bungalow with the bedrooms opening out onto a veranda from where there was a view across the fields to the now shifting and changeable skies.

I found the company tired and rather depressed: something was wrong with everything as usual. I was glad to start work again, though I was thankful to have missed the month in Calcutta.

I saw my first snake at Ranchi — a krait in the hotel garden, which caused a lot of excitement — all the hotel servants and gardeners rushed about banging the flowerbeds with sticks, but the krait eluded them all the same. When I first arrived in India, I had expected snakes to pop their heads out of every drawer I opened, but by now I had got so used not to seeing them that the krait's appearance came as quite a shock.

* * *

After a few performances at the camp theatre in Ranchi, we started touring the neighbouring camps. Some of them were were quite far away so we would not get back until well into the small hours of the morning. Renée was as inexhaustible as ever, and the mess parties became hilarious wherever we went, however stiffly and starchily they started off. There was one terrific Sunday at an RAF mess, which started off with an invitation for drinks at 12.00 a.m. and finished up at about 12.00 p.m. that night.

* * *

And then there was the famous picnic to which a nearby army camp had invited Renée, Joan, Peggy and me. Peggy, perhaps wisely, did not go.

Geoffrey, a round-faced young subaltern, came round to the hotel all agog with excitement and, on the hotel veranda, told us all about his plans for an outing the colonel was allowing him to organize. For the next few days he kept on coming up with fresh plans and ideas, but so far the only thing he seemed to have 'organized' successfully was the drink.

Our destination was to be a waterfall about fifteen miles away. Geoffrey was to take Renée and me in a station bus to meet the colonel and the rest of the officers who were coming too. Joan would be travelling with Geoffrey's friend Peter in his jeep.

Geoffrey's planning broke down from the start when he arrived to fetch us nearly an hour late and then hung about over drinks in the hotel. He had failed to organize any sandwiches, he said, and the hotel could only let him have a few — 'just enough for the colonel', he told us guffawing.

Peter and Joan left some time before Geoffrey got the station bus organized and bumping down the road to our rendezvous with the colonel at a signpost on the way to the falls. It was late for the meeting with them and Geoffrey had had too little foresight to think of bringing a map or finding out the way in advance, so of course we kept going wrong.

Then, when we eventually reached the signpost, Geoffrey failed to notice it and shot straight past with Renée and me yelling at him in unison. I wondered how on earth he had ever passed any courses and thought what a hopeless hash he would make of trying to lead his men anywhere to do anything. We swung round in the road, with Geoffrey nearly sending the station bus into the ditch at each manoeuvre and, with apologetic guffaws, we went back to find the signpost.

Of course, the colonel's party had given up waiting a long time back and neither Joan nor Peter was visible. It was a further ten miles to the falls along a road that was little more than a cart track. In the station bus we were thrown up to the roof and banged down again at each jolt, until we felt that we must be black and blue all over.

It had originally been arranged that the ladies of the party were to be taken on in jeeps from the crossroads. Jeeps are made to travel over rough ground and are far more comfortable to ride in than a badly sprung station bus, but of course we had missed travelling in the jeeps with the colonel.

On either side of the track, the country was wet and jungly. Sometimes streams ran right across in front of us, and in one of these, where there was a steep dip down and rise up, we thought we had got stuck for good and all.

Had we been less exasperated than we were by this time, Renée and I would gladly have heaved Geoffrey into the water. However, with a mighty lurch the station bus rose victorious on the other side and we bounced on our way for another half dozen miles until we reached the falls.

By this time, though, even if we had been going to see Niagara, Renée and I could not have cared less. But once on our feet again, and refreshed by a couple of drinks, we were ready to climb over the rocks to the head of the falls to where the rush of yellow water threw itself over the edge of the cliff to drop into a white froth of uprising foam far away beneath.

Above the falls, the over-swollen river swirled along, hurrying to the edge, gaining momentum as other streams came pouring in to join it, and then in a great rush it went hurtling over into space — a long breath-taking drop, the thundering impact below with foam shooting wildly up into the air, and then the river seemed to shake itself free of the tumult and wound peacefully down the rich green valley and into the distance.

It began to rain, and we turned back for the land, slipping perilously on the rocks.

* * *

Lunch — the colonel's sandwiches — was the next order of the day, but where were we to eat them? The little rest hut with a view over the falls was packed full of Chinese soldiers cooking their meal while squatting on the veranda and carrying on a lusty singsong at the same time.

However, with a case of gin and the colonel's sandwiches, we managed to squeeze into a little back room out of the rain and, given that the rain showed no sign of stopping, there we had to remain. And there the picnic fizzled out to a rather damp conclusion.

* * *

The high-pressure round of parties at the hotel, at the club, or at after-the-show messes carried on all the time we were at Ranchi, accelerating towards the end until it was not only I who was exhausted.

'We do like you so much Renée,' said one young officer, voicing the opinion of quite a few, 'but we are glad you are going.'

This amused Renée enormously. It took more than a nightly show, long drives to the camps and bed at four or five each morning to wear her out.

* * *

Our next port of call was to be Panegar, Mountbatten's

newly built and enormous base camp for the Burma front, where we were to do a one-night stand and then to carry on in the train to Calcutta, from where we were bound — to our great joy — for Darjeeling.

But first there was to be an uncomfortable 36 hours ahead of us.

21

The Show Must Go On: Mountain Railway to Darjeeling and Costumes Lost *en Route*

In the courses of their act together Connie would ask Jack, 'Do you like Panegar [or wherever we happened to be playing that night] as a whole?'

'As a hole yes', he would reply to a burst of applause from the audience, who seemed to relish the joke just as much wherever we went, even in such beautiful places as Murray and Darjeeling.

But if any place deserved to be called a 'hole' on our tour it was Panegar. Right out in the middle of flat monotonous plains, the camp lay in the burning heat, infested with snakes, mosquitoes and every other type of insect.

* * *

The train drew up at Panegar station at about midday and, after an especially hot and dirty journey, we were all longing to leave the carriages as quickly as possible when a large colonel in an imposing white topi came stalking down the platform.

He announced in a loud and strident voice that, given that

we would have to make a very early start the next morning and that since they had no intention of letting us get away early that night, he would suggest we leave everything in the train and return to sleep there.

But we did not see eye to eye with the colonel over this matter. We would prefer to have a few hours sleep in the camp between clean sheets than endure another night in the dirty carriages now being backed into a siding where we would have had neither lights nor fans.

So our luggage was bundled out onto the platform and we piled into waiting staff cars to drive through the newly built 'town' of Panegar. This consisted of army huts surrounded by a wasteland lying in the burning heat and swarming with mosquitoes.

We were transported to various messes for lunch, having to be rationed out as usual in big camps. Connie, Jack and I landed up at that of the Commander of the Royal Engineers.

* * *

It was always difficult for us when we first arrived after a journey. We would be longing for a bath, for something to eat and then to fall into a bed, but instead we would have to sit sipping gin and lime and making conversation for an hour before a meal was served and then have to wait until that was over before being able to relax.

The officer who took us to our rooms after lunch in the mess bungalow apologized to me that there were no blinds or curtains on my window.

'You see, we were really expecting a married couple in here,' he explained politely, though I failed to understand why it would not have mattered who had looked in through the window had my husband been with me.

* * *

We held the show in a great barn of a cinema in which everyone had to shout their loudest to make themselves heard at the back and in which Jack's piano must have sounded like a faint tinkle.

An hour before the curtain rose, Frank arrived to say that Joy was feeling too ill to go on that night. We looked at each other hopelessly. Peggy would be the only one of the 'four girls' left. Quickly we arranged for Peggy to do *Love in a Mist* as a solo, with Connie doing the tap number on her own and I the ballet as a '*pas de seule*' as well as my Mexican dance.

Peggy immediately got down to teaching me the opening number for Jack and the girls, for it would have missed its point had she tried to do that alone. I partly knew the dialogue already, but the dancing was tap and I had never had a tap lesson in my life; still, I somehow bluffed my way through it. The number was called *One Happy Family*, which was slightly misleading as far as our company was concerned, divided as we were into two opposing camps.

Peggy and I were both dropping with exhaustion before even going on that night. And what a hot night it was too, how many thousands of mosquitoes! In the dressing room we had to keep covering ourselves up, however much we were longing to throw everything off.

* * *

The mess party afterwards was lavish, but an appalling effort, and that is all I can remember of it.

After a few hours sleep we were up again and driving to the station, there to search the siding for our coach, which had shunted off somewhere during the night. We stumbled over the railway lines in the semi-darkness to make enquiries from several people who knew nothing, until the railway transport officer at last came to our rescue.

* * *

Later in the day we arrived in Calcutta and once again we were enveloped in the stifling, noisy, railway station atmosphere of the Grand Hotel.

Sitting in the lounge was Jean, the plaster jacket off at last, but not a very cheerful Jean for all that, having just been robbed of all her money. The hotel was a shocking place for thieves. Brenda was to lose a new wristwatch there, and Renée never knew where her things had been stolen — she told us she had lost £100 worth of jewellery altogether on the tour. One ring she was quite sure Shah had taken, though she could not openly accuse him.

* * *

Shah had left us suddenly at Ranchi, saying that he must go back to Kohart because his wife was ill. We all gave him money to help him pay the fare, and off he went. Later we had intelligence that he had merely been taking a holiday in Delhi. Jack, our manager, said he refused to have him back, but when he turned up at the door of the bedroom Renée, Joan and I were sharing at the Grand Hotel, looking unutterably piteous, protesting his innocence, begging to return to us, and finishing up by telling us that his wife had died, we did not know what to say. Although we felt that we could not ever really trust him again, those imploring dark eyes, brimming over with tears gradually melted us.

Jack, however, was not moved and, as the manager, he put his foot down against Shah coming back. So we went off to Darjeeling with only Gulum to 'do' for the whole company.

* * *

On the platform of Calcutta station a positive army of porters lined up to receive their tips after carting our luggage

— twelve lots now because both Brenda as well as Jean were back with us again. The line of dark-faced porters in their uniform of red turbans and short tunics looked, Jean said, like the chorus of a musical comedy.

She got out of the carriage to stand in front of them and shout:

'Come on girls, one, two, three, kick right, kick left!'

The Darjeeling train was very full. All eight of us women were in one compartment intended for five, and the men were in with seven officers, making eleven in all. By the time the eight bedrolls were piled into our carriage, we did not see how we ourselves were ever going to get in, but we managed it somehow and, after all, it was only for one night. I do not know how we ever managed to get ourselves sorted out in the morning, though.

* * *

We tumbled out onto the platform of the junction for the mountain train up to Darjeeling, looking even wilder than usual. We had breakfast at the station and then had to struggle to find seats on the little mountain train waiting in another bay.

We were disappointed that our expedition up the Himalayas had to take place during the rainy season. The clouds lay heavy over the mountains as our train drew nearer towards them across the plain. Soon we plunged into the dark belt of jungle that encircles the foot of the Himalayas, with its high trees, thickly tangled undergrowth and those long hanging roots that Tarzan is so fond of swinging on in the Hollywood jungles.

We were told that the tea planters had hunted here for big game before the war, but the only 'big game' we happened to see were a few monkeys.

The railway track wound its way upwards round the hills, sometimes travelling in zigzags to take us off onto a sidetrack to reverse. We caught glimpses of the views through the mist, of the massive grey shapes above us of the mountains we were climbing, the wet green tea plantations we were passing through, and down below us the jungle, but the clouds were closing in more and more, and the rain was drenching down.

At the little wayside stations, children would come and hang on the railings to watch the train. The children of these hill people were tiny, round-faced and charming. Some of them had baskets of fruit, which they tried to sell to the passengers from the train windows, but hardly any of them whined for *baksheesh*. Some little bare-footed black-eyed boys would cling onto the outside of the train as it left the station and get taken for a ride up the line, rolling off onto the bank when they had had enough.

In places, the track ran very near to the edge of the precipice and this gave us an uncomfortable feeling because Brenda had passed round the news that there had been 'a lot of dirty big landslides up here during the monsoon'.

* * *

We arrived at Darjeeling in a blanket of mist and saw nothing of it at all. The married couples went to a hotel, the women in the company to the very pleasant and well-run YWCA; Renée and Joan treated themselves to a week at the Mount Everest Hotel.

I cannot pretend that our week in Darjeeling was a success from the theatrical point of view, for we gave only one performance there to a convalescent home just before we came away.

The truck containing all the props and costumes had got lost on the journey from Panegar and, given that it had been lying in a railway yard in Calcutta, it was not discovered for several days. Then it had to be sent on and brought up by the mountain railway. Jack kept sending telegrams in all directions and later wired ENSA to ask if we could stay on for an extra few days to give at least a couple of shows to justify our visit to Darjeeling.

But the Calcutta office wanted us back, to be on time at Dacca, our next destination. The manager of the Darjeeling cinema, where we were booked to play, was so annoyed about having our first performance postponed from day to day that he had lost interest in the show.

So we just had a week's holiday, though the worry over the trunk and answering endless questions from people who wanted to know when we would be starting really prevented us from enjoying it as such. But how beautiful it was up there at Darjeeling when the mists cleared and the shapes of the mountains broke into view and rose towering up across the valleys.

* * *

I met a young lieutenant at a party who shared my longing to walk and explore the country and together we climbed the hill above the town for a sight of Kunchinjunga, and on another day we took a long walk over the hills to a Buddhist monastery.

From the point above the town Kunchinjunga remained obstinately behind the clouds. There was a Hindu shrine built up there where little ragged flags covered in prayers hung from tall posts all round it and the shrine itself was sprinkled with red dust. The Hindus always paint their shrines and temples with red, which is a symbol of menstruation and a part of their worship of fertility.

The visit we made later on to the Buddhist monastery was exciting, but we were slightly disappointed because it was obvious that they had a constant stream of visitors there and as a result the place had become rather commercialized. Their religion was not pure Buddhism, either, but mixed with traces of Hinduism.

The interior of the temple, with a gigantic brass Buddha dominating one wall and cases filled with other smaller Buddhas, Hindu gods, great animal and other devilish-looking masks staring down at you from every side, was, however, quite overpowering. The walls and ceiling of the temple were thickly painted in the brightest, gaudiest colours and, wherever you turned, there was no reposeful spot on which to rest your eyes.

The monks sat on the floor in two rows in front of the great Buddha. They had prayer books before them, piles of closely written leaves that were not sewn together. They were all chanting out loud, each in his own individual way, going at his own pace and not attempting to keep time with the others. When one had finished the prayer on the top leaf, that leaf was placed at the bottom of the pile and the next leaf was started on. We noticed that they were not too intent on their prayers to resist taking a good look to see how much we were putting in the box by the door.

* * *

From the monastery we set out on the long walk back to Darjeeling, stopping for refreshments at a wayside guest-house where, to our great surprise and delight, we were served with a real Scottish tea consisting of baps, scones and shortcake. It seemed to add to the incongruity of a Scottish tea in the Himalayas that an enormous Negro should be sprawling on the grass outside in the garden.

While sitting by the window having tea, the sky suddenly seemed to break open and I had my first sight of Kunchinjunga with its dazzling white peaks hanging in the air. It was a breathtaking and exquisitely beautiful moment. When the clouds drew over the peaks again, I could hardly believe what I had just seen, that it was possible for Kunchinjunga to tower over the world like that, until it reappeared again and I gasped with wonder. It was so godlike and so remote that I felt a rush of gladness that Kunchinjunga was still unconquerable, unsoiled by the human touch.

Of course, we hatched a lot of plans to go to Tiger Hill one day in an attempt to see Everest, but when we heard that we would have to get up at three o'clock if we were to be on Tiger Hill by dawn and took into account the heavy cost of a taxi and the 100 to 1 chance that Everest would remain hidden during the monsoon, our plans petered out and came to nothing.

* * *

Needless to say, we went to all the usual parties and dances up at Darjeeling.

At one dance, held in the lovely galleried ballroom of the club, a stray partner in the Paul Jones told me that the Allies had taken back Paris, beautiful Paris, which one so dreaded hearing may be in ruins — 'they practically handed it over, unharmed,' he said. At the finish of the dance, the band played the Marseillaise and there was a buzz of excited whispering and questioning among those who had not yet heard the news. Then everybody streamed out into the keen night air to sail down the hillside in a fleet of rickshaws.

* * *

There were some wild parties that week at the Mount Everest Hotel. With Renée at a party, it was guaranteed to be lively and original. At one of these parties, the guests poured brandy into their soup plates, and ladled it down with spoons and at another the women played cards against the men, trying to get the clothes off each other's backs.

So the week at Darjeeling came to an end with our one solitary performance at the convalescent home, which made us all feel a little ashamed, and then we had to return to the steaming plain, the wet oven of Calcutta, and the stewpot of the Grand Hotel. As I had started to feel ill, I went to bed on arrival and stayed there until we had to leave for Dacca. Rotten as I felt, and furious with myself at the thought of perhaps developing something and being out of the show again, it was still a relief to me not to have to go down for meals into the steaming crowded Black Hole of Calcutta — in other words the dining room below.

22

Up the Brahmaputra: By River to Dacca and Down with Jaundice

Our journey to Dacca was to be made partly by train and partly by riverboat up the great Brahmaputra River, and it was to this half of the journey that we were all looking forward. Dacca would be the furthest east, and the nearest to Assam that we would be travelling — transport for a large company became too difficult after that.

We reached the end of the train journey from Calcutta in the early hours of the morning and bundled out of the carriages to wait, for what seemed like hours, sitting on piles of luggage on the dirty platform until it was time to go aboard the riverboat. Feeling by now utterly ill and miserable, I curled myself up on a trunk, not caring what happened.

At last came the signal to move and we trudged off down the platform between little groups of squatting Indians, the Walbahs, with their trays of native food being passed from group to group and the half naked bodies of children strewn about for anyone to tread on.

It was pleasant to step aboard the boat with the sound of the river lapping down below and the cool breeze blowing against one's cheek. It was a sturdy little vessel, squat in shape, with a promenade deck running round the first-class dining saloon and eight little cabins leading off on either side. The people down below in the steerage were crowded together like flies over jam. Upstairs, everyone was sitting down to a meal — everyone, that is, except me. I went straight to one of the cabins allotted to our company and dropped onto the bunk. Lying there, I felt the steady gliding motion of the boat underneath me as it left the shore and moved off down the river, so silently and peacefully after the long hours spent in the shaking train and the miserable wait lying on cases on the noisy platform.

* * *

The next morning, we awoke to look out of the cabin windows at the great swollen Brahmaputra, spreading its vast wastes of grey and yellow water to the lush vegetation of the opposite shore. When we kept close into land on one side, the other shore was barely visible, such a tremendous breadth of river flowed between.

Ten to twelve hours later, we arrived at the river port and were met as usual by a staff officer who told us that he had transport 'laid on' outside to take us to Dacca.

* * *

The little town at which we had arrived was appallingly over-populated with malnutrition, poverty and wretchedness laid completely bare. We then drove out onto a road running alongside the river and bordered by rice fields on the other side and, after a couple of miles or so, were entering Dacca itself, which was as over-populated, filthy and miserable as the former place had been.

'You'd better shut your eyes while passing through Dacca,' our staff officer told us.

Our billets at Dacca were to be in part of a convalescent home. We drove through high gates into a pleasant stretch of parkland, with one or two fair-sized lakes, and drew up before a long wooden bungalow, with the usual veranda in front. The rooms were bare, furnished with just army beds, and we were several in each room, but it was on the whole much better than we had expected from Dacca.

I went straight to bed and Jack sent for a doctor. When he arrived, I was told that I had jaundice and had better go straight into hospital.

'For how long?' I wanted to know, sickened at the thought of being out of the show again.

'Jaundice takes three weeks,' replied the doctor.

* * *

We were to be giving performances in Dacca for ten days, and then we would be due to travel back across India to Bombay to wait for a ship to the Middle East, filling in with dates in the meanwhile.

I swore that I was not going to remain in hospital for three weeks and let the others go without me, not now that our time was nearly up and Cairo was waiting for me across the sea. I was coming out of that hospital at the end of ten days and travelling with them, doctor's orders or no doctor's orders.

Fortunately for me, the colonel at the hospital was an easy-going man who did not stand in the way of my leaving after ten days, so I did not have to fight my way out.

* * *

I will skim very quickly over that tedious time in the Seventeenth British Hospital. The wards were all half open to the elements and I was put in the sole women's ward with a couple of the hospital sisters, one suffering from jaundice, the other, a large and buxom lady, from malaria. The former I recognized as having been on the *Marnix*, or rather I believe she recognized me first. They both made pleasant companions, but in my state of impatience, the hours seemed to drag by intolerably, especially in the evenings when the heavy khaki mosquito nets were lowered and, given that the ward was lit only by hurricane lamps, we could not see enough to sew or read but were condemned to lie in a khaki gloom, while the insects buzzed around the hanging lamps outside and the frogs croaked across the damp concrete floor.

The sister who had been on board the *Marnix* told me of the hardships of the life she had led in wartime, the length of service required of them and the long hours they had to work, sometimes in the worst climates. She had previously been in West Africa, which is one of the most trying climates for women.

She amused me by singing one of the songs of the British soldiers stationed on the West African coast, 'I'm Dreaming of a White Mistress'.

✷ ✷ ✷

Of course the members of the company came in to visit me and to report on the show, which seemed to be going down as well as usual — not that I really liked to hear of it going down quite so well when I was out of it. But they were all fed up with Dacca. Life was not much of a picnic in the bungalow. There was no servant to keep the place clean, and Gulum, our one and solitary bearer, was doing the cooking and practically everything else on top of his own work of looking after the stage wardrobe. They were short of water and the bathroom was swarming with cockroaches.

One morning, several of them had gone for a bathe in the lake. They had spent at least a couple of hours in the water, splashing about and enjoying themselves, but quite oblivious that about a hundred naked soldiers, who had been just about to enter the water when they arrived, were hiding in the bushes all round the lake, too embarrassed to emerge.

* * *

My ten days were up at last, and I left the hospital, feeling like a prisoner released from gaol. An ambulance took me to the bungalow to join the others, who were in various stages of getting ready, packing and having breakfast. Gulum, sweating and exhausted, was trudging backwards and for-wards from the bungalow to the waiting lorry, weighed down with luggage. I noticed the Indian driver of the vehicle standing by doing nothing and, with gestures, suggested he should lend Gulum a hand. He turned on me a face of the greatest indignation and disgust and did not move a limb. I had forgotten about the inhuman rigidity of the caste system.

* * *

The staff officer who had met us off the boat on our arrival drove us back to catch the returning boat that morning. I sat in the front seat beside him and had quite a heated quarrel with him over a pye-dog, which he nearly ran over on the road. I asked him why he had not slowed down and he replied that 'there were far too many pye-dogs around and that they needed killing off.'

'Well then shoot them dead,' I said, 'Don't just knock them down, and leave them on the roadside, perhaps in agony, for hours.'

'Oh you're too soft-hearted,' he said. 'Life is cheap in India — all life,' and he went on to talk about the Bengal famine and how the idiotic Indians had preferred to starve rather than touch the contaminated European food that the army had offered them.

'All right then, idiotic,' I said, 'but can't you see anything noble in their preferring to die rather than violate their faith?'

'Oh death means nothing to them, life is cheap out here'.

'Your ideas are cheap, you mean,' I said.

* * *

There were to be several hitches on our way back to Calcutta. First, we were told that the boat we should have been travelling on had been grounded on a sandbank up the river and that we would have to wait for another one. So we were taken to the club where we hung about for half the day before going on board after lunch.

It was pleasant sitting on deck, gliding along through the late afternoon, watching the native crafts bobbing on the water, and the richly green river bank slipping by while the sun went slowly down in a pink and crimson sky, flushing the transparent ripples of the water.

Darkness came and we moved into the saloon for dinner. Somehow or other we had become a party. A couple of officers on board had seen the show at one or other of our venues and had reintroduced themselves. Others had tacked on, so here again we were back in the old atmosphere of whiskies and sodas, and 'What will you have?' and 'What do you think of India?'

* * *

Suddenly there was a jolt throughout the boat, which reminded Joan and me unpleasantly of the *Marnix*. We were stuck on a sandbank. Time went by while efforts were made to get us off again. Then the engines stopped and the attempts were abandoned. How long might we have to remain there? Until the following morning at least, when the next boat would come down the river. Of course we would miss the train connection and our reserved compartments to

Calcutta, there would be no breakfast for anybody on board and there were only eight cabins to be shared by everybody for the night. Still, there was nothing to do but to lump it. Renée announced gaily that we would keep the party going all night, and she, for one, did not want to sleep. However, they insisted on my taking one of the bunks, though I insisted too on each of us having rests in turn. But after a few hours, to everyone's surprise, the current drifted us off the sandbank again, and everyone started speculating as to whether or not we would be in time to catch the midnight train to Calcutta.

It did not worry me whether we caught the train or not, for I was in no hurry to get back to Calcutta and to the Grand Hotel. We were there quite soon enough, and I retired to bed for the couple of days' break before travelling on to Bombay.

* * *

The Grand Hotel was as crowded and noisy as ever, so I was thankful to be upstairs and away from it all. I sat up in bed peacefully reading Naomi Jacob's *White Wool* and knitting myself a cardigan. A knock came at the door, and there were a couple of American sergeants looking for Jean, with whom I was sharing the room. Jean was not there, so they stayed on.

'You read *White Wool* and you knit white wool,' remarked one of them, 'Say lady, you're in a rut.'

They would not believe that I was recovering from jaundice, and teased me for hours to go downstairs and dance. Neither would they believe that I must not touch alcohol, but went all the way downstairs to bring me up some sherry, which they later drank.

The following day, one of them returned and sat at my bedside from eleven in the morning until five in the evening. I was nearly at screaming pitch, but when he kept saying, grinning all over his face, how he had hardly spoken to a 'dame' for two years, and how 'swell' it was doing so, I had not the heart to turn him away.

I did think that I would be rewarded though when he mentioned some beautiful South American stockings he had bought for his wife.

'But now she writes she wants a divorce, and she's not going to get them,' he said. But he had left them 'way back at the "drome"', so it was clear that was I not going to get them either.

This story reminded me of a British officer Renée met at a camp who boasted to her about the superb stockings he had bought for his wife, which he intended to take home with him when he returned to England.

'But why don't you send them?' Renée had suggested. 'Everyone is so badly in need of stockings in England these days.'

'What?' the fond husband replied. 'Send her home stockings so that other men can admire her wearing them? Not bloody likely!'

* * *

We were soon on the train for Bombay, this time a main line express with clean carriages and meals laid on.

Gulum informed us, from a conversation with a general's bearer he had met on Calcutta platform, that there would be a ship leaving almost as soon as we arrived in Bombay — in fact he gave us the exact date. This news gave us a bit of a shock. Could any security exist in India when native servants on one side of the country knew all about the movements of ships in and out of ports on the other side?

And Gulum was perfectly right, too, though our company failed to organize bookings for us on that particular ship. The office refused to apply for our passages until we were all back in Bombay; consequently, we did not actually leave until three weeks later and, in the meanwhile, were sent off to Poona, only two hours away by rail, to continue giving shows until we were suddenly recalled.

23

The Curtain Drops at Poona: Final Performances, a Trip to the Races

We had two camps to play to on the way to Poona and, because there was no accommodation for us at either place, the news was broken to us that, for the couple of days in question, we would just have to live in the railway coach on a siding and have our meals in the station dining room. This did not sound like much fun, for by this time we were all heartily sick of spending our days on trains and railway platforms. However, when we eventually saw the special travelling coach in which the ENSA authorities said that all the companies would soon be touring India, we cheered up enormously.

* * *

As the office had reached the conclusion that small companies were best for India, the coach was designed to accommodate eight people. There were four little cabins, neatly fitted out with two bunks in each, a bathroom, and a small sitting room with a tiny kitchen leading out of it. As there were 12 of us, the four men slept in the sitting room on camp beds.

But we felt hot and dirty being drawn up in a railway

siding all day long. We pulled down the blinds, lay on our bunks and tried to sleep until it was time to get ready to go to the camp for dinner.

We had all been invited to a meal before the show. It was to be the army that night and the air force the following evening. The army certainly treated us very well, for they served us dinner before the show and drinks afterwards.

* * *

That evening I talked to a dark, bony-faced officer who told me that he was pondering in his mind whether to go into a Tibetan monastery after the war, to carry on with his studies in psychology, or to stay on in India to work among the people there. The Indian character and mentality interested him enormously.

He told me how he had studied Urdu and how he often went among the Indians, disguised as one of them and virtually inconspicuous because of his lean darkness.

It was refreshing to talk to someone who could see beyond the 'lot of dirty wogs' attitude.

* * *

The RAF upstaged the army the following day by sending us an invitation in the morning for lunch at its mess. We accepted, though if we had realized how long the motor journey was going to be over an appalling road, which we had to do again there and back in the evening, we might have hesitated.

They seemed rather stiff and slow when we first arrived, but they livened up in the evening at the party after the show, which carried on until three or four in the morning. We also spent time in the other ranks' mess, so it was a full day. The camp was situated on a green plain encircled by strange, fantastically shaped hills. Although not a great distance from either Poona or Bombay, it was too far for us to get into either town very often, so in both camps we found the men bored and weary, and much appreciative of the entertainment. We had a spirited party that night at which the RAF produced a 'line' book, in which every 'line' that happened to be 'shot' was recorded with one signature witnessed by another. One of the best I can remember was — 'no, I don't listen to the news, I make it.'

* * *

Then we moved on to Poona. Poona, the 'pukka' town of India, the famous name, pompously rolled off the tongues of many a mahogany-faced retired colonel in his West End club, or his falsely whiskered imitator in the music halls. Well, I am afraid my first impression of Poona was that it was a thoroughly suburban place, with long trim rows of neat and respectable bungalows surrounded by well-kept flowerbeds. The name 'Colonel This' or 'Brigadier That' was printed on the garden gate of each house, which I regarded as a delightful touch of Poona snobbery. Nobody below the rank of major would of course dare to put his name up, though it struck me that it would have been fun to erect an enormous mansion and proudly display 'Private Smith' on a placard outside the entrance. Then there was the Poona club, the Poona racecourse, the Poona cricket club and the turf club, which we were to visit later on and which were all very pukka and pleasant.

* * *

I liked the main shopping street; it was strongly native in character and had a charm of its own. This was southern India and the difference in atmosphere between it and the north was immediately perceptible. One sight we had never seen before was of yogis sitting at the roadside, their eyes fixed on a square of white material spread out on the ground in front of them and so lost in contemplation that a car might swerve within an inch of their starched turbans without their moving a muscle.

* * *

Sid, the officer to be in charge of the company during our time in the district, met us on our arrival at Poona station. Afterwards, he used to enjoy giving imitations of the gracious way in which we had received him. As he put it, 'on catching sight of me a lot of snooty faces at the window leant out and demanded in chorus, "any post?" then retired again disgruntled.'

We were all feeling rather disgruntled over a rumour that had got around that we were to go on living in our railway coach siding for the whole indefinite period that we would be in Poona. However, Sid was able to reassure us on that point, though he told us it had been a job to find billets for all of us. We were to be spread out at different hotels and private houses, with Ivan and Jack at an officers' club. I was to be at one of the hotels, but Renée, who had been put down as a guest at one of the private houses, asked me to change with her.

'I don't want to have to behave, you know Catharine,' she said.

* * *

I was rather pleased to change over, especially once I had met my very pleasant host and hostess, and seen my comfortable bedroom, opening out onto a shady veranda with flower gardens below. My host, Mr F, an important personage in the Indian Police, was of course entitled to have his name on his gate. His wife was head of the Poona Women's Voluntary Service and she went off early each morning to her office attired in a most becoming light blue uniform. Although their bungalow was large and furnished both tastefully and comfortably, it still had the same tin baths and poor sanitation that were found elsewhere.

I found staying with this kind elderly couple very restful, though I only really saw them at meal times because Mrs F was at her office in the mornings and Sid collected me every afternoon and did not bring me home until after they had both retired to bed.

Mr F was a cheery-looking old man who would come out at meal times with remarks such as, 'Parliament is made up of a lot of swindlers.' His wife would look solemnly across the table at him and say, 'I don't think you can go as far as that dear!'

Poor Mrs F became very upset at the news from England that Elsie and Doris Waters (Gert and Daisy), who had just returned from their Indian tour with ENSA, were 'saying things' in the papers about how little the Poona ladies were doing for the war effort and generally poking fun at them. Mrs F was incapable of realizing that the temptation to laugh at the Poona ladies was obviously too strong for two music-hall artists such as Gert and Daisy to resist. She immediately had a photograph taken of rows upon rows of uniformed Poona womanhood representing this, that or the other, which she was sending straight back to England to be plastered over the front pages of every newspaper in circulation.

※　※　※

Our time of waiting in Poona stretched out to three weeks. They were three weeks of hard work, too, for we had to make some very long journeys and got no days off. Our transport consisted of fifteen-hundredweight trucks (rather a come down for Poona, we thought), though we were given basket chairs, which stood in the back, and so we were fairly comfortable except when travelling over very bumpy roads. On one long journey, at the other end of which we were put up for the night in private houses because of the distance, we all got so filthy from the clouds of dust blowing up from the road as we were sitting in the back of our fifteen-hundredweight trucks that we arrived looking like nothing on earth. Joan and I felt quite ashamed of turning up in this state at the smart-looking bungalow where a colonel and his wife were accommodating us for the night.

After a cup of tea with the colonel and his wife, we retired to the bathroom where two tin baths were ready, filled and waiting for us side by side. We scrambled thankfully in and watched the water getting blacker and blacker as we scrubbed ourselves down.

* * *

The whole company was now together again at last and we were pleased to be able to finish up with the show as it should be. We had rehearsed the ballet and put it back in the repetoire for the first performance in Poona. I believe we only put on two performances in the actual town and one at a hospital, which was a very sad occasion.

Every one was coming off the stage, complaining bitterly at the flatness of the audience, who were not laughing at anything.

'You can't blame them', said a soldier stagehand quietly. 'They are all very seriously consumptive out there, and it hurts them too much to laugh.' We felt sick with pity and found it very difficult to keep up the light-hearted touch until the end of that performance.

* * *

Some of the old Mard Island crowd turned up at Poona, so naturally various meetings and parties were organized. One

Sunday we went for a picnic into the green, hilly and very attractive countryside beyond the outskirts of Poona. It was certainly a better-organized picnic than the one to the waterfall from Ranchi, despite setting out at about one o'clock when the original plan was to leave at eleven and one of the cars breaking down on the way. The car ahead came hurrying back to the rescue while the other dilapidated-looking object was left in a ditch at the side of the road.

* * *

We were now climbing up into the hills. Down below lay a huge grass enclosure, surrounded by colossal high walls, which one member of our party said had been an elephant run belonging to some Indian princes.

At the top of the hill we piled out, found comfortable seats on the grass in the shade, opened up our hampers and started to gnaw on our chicken bones.

After lunch, we started playing a game of 'truths'. 'Truths' is fun only if people have no scruples at all about what questions they ask and stick to the exact truth in their answers. This particular game, in which everyone was trying to pry as much as possible into everyone else's love affairs, became pretty frank, though I do not think anyone's feelings were mortally wounded or any relations were seriously damaged.

It was nearly sunset by the time we had all squeezed into the one remaining car to go back to Poona. It took us some time to get going because Renée was insisting on travelling back sitting on the running board with her back against the mudguard, and the driver and owner of the car was not going to budge an inch with her there.

* * *

The Curtain Drops at Poona: Final Performances

I wanted to go to the races while I was in Poona and so changed an invitation to the cinema one Saturday afternoon into one to the racecourse instead. I met my escort for lunch at an excellent Chinese restaurant, which we left feeling as full as one always does after a Chinese meal. In the road outside, a couple of Indians with a basket of cobras were clamouring to show the *sahib* and *memsahib* the genuine Indian rope trick. I wanted to stay and watch, but the *sahib* had money on the first race and he was panting to be there to see it.

Poona racecourse is very attractive with its wide sweep of track stretching away to the blue hills on the horizon. Inside the enclosures on the beautifully kept velvety grass, Indian women in wonderfully colourful saris floated like butterflies among gigantic banks of flowers. We went down to the paddock to watch the horses, many of them magnificent-looking Arabs, with flowing manes and compact vigorous bodies, passing round in a circle. An Arab horse owner, a patriarchal figure in long flowing robes, sat with king-like dignity in the background as the crowd pressed against the railings, intently watching the horses as they passed by. We squeezed our way through to the front and the *sahib* pointed out the horse he had been tipped to back. I picked out the horse that seemed to me to move the best and backed it with five rupees.

Well, I was lucky, and the *sahib* was not. On the three races I had time to see before leaving to go and get ready for Sid and the fifteen-hundredweight truck at five o'clock, I had won 43 rupees, more than three pounds, but the *sahib* was well down on his luck and I left him in a not too good temper, but for me the afternoon had been most enjoyable, with a nice little *baksheesh* thrown in.

* * *

The governor of Bombay happened to be at his Poona

residence while we were there, so I got in touch with my brother's friend Michael. He came over by car, with one of the other ADCs and took Joan and me off to Government House for a swim in the lovely natural pool in the grounds and for tea afterwards in the ADC's bungalow.

The pool was deep and clean, with rocky sides and bottom. We swam from patches of water warmed by the sun, into deliciously cool ones, and then climbed out of the water into a little flat-bottomed boat to rest. We lazily paddled and drifted about, until the boat gradually filled up with water and submerged, plunging us all in again to the delicious coolness below.

At the gates of Government House I saw a cobra for the first time. It came wriggling across the entrance with amazing rapidity, flashing like glass in the sunlight. Michael was out of the car in a second and, to our astonishment, horror and amusement, he started jumping on the cobra with a yell of excitement. The lodge keeper then came running out with a stick.

'It might easily have bitten your ankle,' I said to Michael in the car afterwards.

'I suppose it might,' he answered cheerfully.

I wanted Michael to get us all invitations for the coming ball at Government House and he did his best, but was unsuccessful. Only a fixed number of ladies and gentlemen might be invited to Government House balls and, given that the correct number of ladies had already accepted, no invitations would be issued for ENSA.

Anyhow, Michael told us that the dances were very stiff formal affairs and we were well out of it. Still, it would have been gloriously 'Poonaish' to go to one.

24

The Return to Cairo and to my Husband

Bombay was very crowded at that time and the ENSA authorities had difficulty trying to squeeze us in anywhere. Until we left for Poona, a newly arrived party of ENSA artists had had to remain on board their ship because there was nowhere to accommodate them. A couple of them, however, had been given a room at the Cecil Hotel where Jean and I had been fixed up for three days.

Jean came to me one morning, laughing.

'Our friends are very obviously just out from England,' she told me. 'One of them said to me this morning, 'Do you think this hotel is all right? I am covered in bites and a cockroach actually ran across the floor yesterday.'

We had a good laugh and wished them luck for their future of bugs, mosquitoes, flying cockroaches and a lot more besides.

* * *

While in Bombay this time, Peggy, Brenda, Jean and I were given an enormous room at the Taj Mahal Hotel. Much as I have always hated sleeping more than two to a room, this time it was fun, for I enjoyed the luxurious feeling of strolling down the great staircase to the vast and shining dining hall below for breakfast and at night watching the lights over the harbour from the front windows of the lounge. They glittered enticingly across the window, making me long to follow them and put out to sea.

* * *

Perhaps I was the only member of the company to be entirely happy about leaving. Several of the others had wanted to stay on in India, but unless the whole company stayed, they were not needed. One or two had formed personal attachments and there were wires sent off at the last minute saying such things as, 'LEAVING: GET HERE IF YOU CAN AND SOON.' But the senders were unfortunately disappointed. Various people were already making plans to return 'sometime' in some other show. I myself did not share their sentiments. Much as I had enjoyed my time in India, and wonderful as so much of it had been, seven months in the country had been long enough for me and I was longing to be back with my husband again and in Cairo, which to me now spelt 'home'.

* * *

We were disappointed at the first sight of our ship at the dockside, for it looked grimy and uninviting. We were also not greatly consoled to find that all the women in the company had to sleep in one cabin, with a Russian, Persian and Palestinian thrown in.

Two double-berthed cabins had been knocked into one and six extra bunks squeezed in. There was scarcely room to swing a cat and we had to take turns getting up and dressing. The Palestinian wanted to bring her cabin trunk in, but we were all quite firm about turning it out and having it sent down to the baggage room with the rest of our luggage. The men were far more fortunate, being only four in a cabin, which had doors opening out onto the deck that they could leave open at night. For us down below, the portholes were securely fastened down as usual.

While we were taking it in turns to unpack on our first afternoon on board — three at a time was the only possible way; the others had either to stay put in their bunks or clear out — when Renée, who had been in rather a highly strung state all day, suddenly flopped to the floor in a dead faint. We got her up on her bunk and sent for the ship's doctor who diagnosed malaria.

'I am expecting at least thirty cases to break out during this voyage,' he said unconcernedly, 'but this one is certainly very prompt.'

* * *

There were a good many Indian troops on board, crowded on the lower decks. A sardine-like existence was nothing new to them, of course, and their officers told us how excited they were at seeing the sea for the first time.

'Where does it all come from?' was one of the most persistent questions they asked, and 'to where does it all go?'

The rest of the passengers aboard this ex-merchantman consisted of a jumble of mixed-race and Indian nurses, a few RAF officers and men, and a number of refugees bound for Palestine from a camp in India. The officers told us that they had felt great indignation over the refugees having been given room on board when RAF personnel, due to return home, had been refused passages. The refugees were a pathetic lot for the most part, resigned and shabby, crowding meekly together on the seats on deck.

* * *

Meal times were rather formal. The 'ladies' of ENSA were divided into two groups — those at the captain's table with

187

OC Troops and the ship's doctor to entertain and the remainder at the chief engineer's, a weather-beaten, blue-eyed old salt. It fell to Peggy and me to make conversation with old 'Chiefy', as he was called, and to the chief gunnery officer, whom we found very heavy going. Peggy told me how he had invited her to his cabin one evening for a drink. While he sat there, dumb as a post, Peggy struggled on valiantly, trying first this topic of conversation and then that, but meeting with a heavy wall of silence. Finally, she gave up making an effort and just sat back sipping her whisky. All at once the the chief gunnery officer broke his silence with:

'How about a little kiss?'

* * *

Brenda, Joan and I soon decided that sleeping ten, or now nine because Renée had been taken away, in so tiny a cabin with the portholes shut was a sheer impossibility. Although the summer was nearly over, the Indian Ocean and the Red Sea are very hot spots even in October, and the temperature was even higher than it had been when we came out in March and nearly collapsed giving that memorable performance on the *City of Exeter*. After a whole summer spent in India, it felt cooler now than it had done then, but it was a lot too hot for sleeping nine in a cabin. We decided that the deck would be the only place.

We had no difficulty borrowing camp beds and sleeping bags and were all fixed up when we heard that the order had gone forth.

'No women to sleep on deck.'

I went straight to the OC Troops, a rather oily and insincere individual with shifty eyes behind his tinted glasses. I spoke to him for half an hour, smiling as sweetly as I could, though I felt like doing something very different, but it was all to no avail.

'The captain does not want the ladies to sleep out on deck,' was the only answer I got.

'What is all the fuss about? I always sleep with my porthole shut.'

'Yes', I said, 'you are in a cabin alone, not squashed in with eight others.'

'But I would be only too pleased to share a cabin with eight ladies,' he sniggered.

I went away in disgust, and my temper was not further improved by being called a fool by Brenda for having asked permission at all.

'I'm just sleeping out,' she said, 'I haven't heard the rule.'

So she and Joan slept out and I slept in the cabin, but the next night I defied the captain and the OC Troops and joined them, and we got away with it for the rest of the voyage.

Later I was told that the captain had considered that we might present the men with too much of a temptation by sleeping up on deck. He was a tight-lipped prim little Scotsman who probably had puritanical ideas about stage artists and considered us all to be children of the devil.

* * *

There was talk of our putting on a show during the voyage, but it never came to anything. To begin with, we had neither Jack nor Connie with us and Renée was laid up. Furthermore, nearly all our costumes had been left in the wardrobe at Bombay. Then there was no suitable place to give a show. The dining saloon was small and an awkward shape, and the decks were all too long and narrow.

So we spent an idle ten days sailing back across the calm blue Indian Ocean.

We spent one night berthed in Aden harbour, with the harbour lights shining mysteriously across the dark water, and left again in the morning when the sunlight was already whitening the rocky hills behind the town and the vast stretches of sand beyond the bay.

Now we were back in the Red Sea again with its crimson glow on the water at sunset, and once more we passed the dozen isolated and unexpected shapes of the islands of the Twelve Apostles.

* * *

There was very little 'doing' on board during this voyage. With passengers of such mixed cultures, it would have been difficult to have made a success of a 'brain's trust', or of an evening's 'housey-housey'.

Though we spent a lot of time with our RAF friends, as the voyage progressed we found ourselves becoming more and more friendly with the ship's officers.

There was Jimmy Darling, known as 'Ducky' (the first mate), Ginger (the second mate) — who was to fall so violently in love with Renée as soon as she was well enough to be fallen for — and the blue-eyed young third mate, Tony.

They would invite us up to their respective cabins. So there would be Brenda having tea with Jimmy and in the next cabin Renée helping Ginger to put away his whisky. I would be next door to them taking tea or playing cribbage with Ducky and next door again Tony would be playing host to Peggy. Joan, meanwhile, would be downstairs in the doctor's cabin sitting for her portrait and Jean, as usual, sunbathing on deck with the ever-faithful Ivan as company.

Ducky and I got on very well, he having a wife and I a husband with whom we did not mind admitting we were in love.

* * *

Every morning, Peggy and I had a standing invitation to a

mug of tea with the gunners, so each day we went along at eleven o'clock and, sitting on the edge of a bunk, sipped tea from large enamel mugs and chatted to Jock, Taffy, George and whoever else happened to be off duty that morning.

One day I happened to mention that it was nearly my wedding anniversary.

'Well, fancy that, luv,' said Jock, 'it's nearly mine too.'

'What date were you married, then?' I said.

'Now let me see,' mumbled Jock, 'the kid now, when was she born?' Then, turning to me with the broadest of grins, 'it was one of the "hooried oop" sort of marriages, you see Catharine.'

* * *

The last day on board came, with invitations to the captain's cabin for farewell drinks. I went up with Joan and Renée, who were teasing me all the time about the way I kept looking at my watch and asking when we would be getting into port.

'But we won't be allowed off the ship for several days you know,' Joan would tell me, and then Renée would say that the captain had just told her that the ship had been delayed and we would not be in port until the next week.

* * *

But Egypt was now in sight and the entrance to the Suez Canal lay in front of our eyes, with Tewfic stretching away to our left. King Farouk's yacht, new, white and streamlined, lay idly in the blue water. As we drew near the quayside, my heart leapt with joy to see again the Egyptian dirty *gallabiyeh*s and red *tarbush*es — this to me was coming home.

Later, in the train, passing through the desert country on the way to Cairo, with the sun beating down on the sand

and the dust beating in through the windows, my spirits soared higher than ever, and the others in the carriage all began to pretend that they too were going to meet their husbands, and kept whispering behind their hands to each other, looking at their watches and jumping up and down in imitation of me.

* * *

Our tour was over. Soon now we were to break up and all go our different ways, Frank and Joy Powell to a Middle East musical production, Ivan and Jean to join a 'straight' drama company. Renée was to return to London and to produce a show there with her husband to take out to the European second front, with Joan, Brenda, Peggy and 'Speedy', a stage manager in the company. They invited me to come along too, but were not surprised that I wanted to stay in the Middle East.

Partings are a sad, but inevitable part of a stage life, where companies are continually breaking up and every show must have an end sometime. But new friends and adventures always lie ahead.

* * *

After a fortnight spent in Cairo I joined Café Continental in Palestine. I was the only English member of the company, who were otherwise all Jewish.

Palestine is an exquisitely beautiful little country, truly a Holy Land, but to describe the tour there and in Syria, until I left the company to await the birth of our son in Cairo, would be another story, and this one is long enough.

* * *

Perhaps, though, I will finish this last chapter with a little story told me by a young Jewish woman in the company, who had been a member of one of the very first ENSA parties to cross over the Trans-Jordan frontier.

The busload of women was kept waiting and waiting while the Arab frontier officials looked them up and down, talked among themselves, disappeared and reappeared. Eventually one of them approached the manager of the party:

'We'll give you forty sheep for the lot,' he said.

Index

Index

Waters, Doris, 146, 180
Waters, Elsie, 146, 180
West End, 11, 68, 104,
   178
Western Desert, 47
Wheeler, Sir Mortimer
   (Rik), 76, 78–9, 82,
   85–6, 89–90
Whitehall Theatre
   (London), 3

Willingdon (Bombay),
   93
Woffington, Peg, 6
Women's Voluntary
   Service, 179

Yorkshire, 9

Zulfigar, 52–3
Zulfigar Palace, 61